GLOBALVIEWPOINTS

Unemployment

Other Books of Related Interest:

At Issue Series
Is China's Economic Growth a Threat to America?

Current Controversies Series
Poverty and Homelessness

Introducing Issues with Opposing Viewpoints Series
Homelessness

Human Rights

Issues That Concern You Series
Career and Technical Education

Opposing Viewpoints Series
The Aging Population

Civil Liberties

Education

Multiracial America

GLOBALVIEWPOINTS

Unemployment

Noël Merino, Book Editor

GREENHAVEN PRESS
A part of Gale, Cengage Learning

GALE
CENGAGE Learning·

Farmington Hills, Mich • San Francisco • New York • Waterville, Maine
Meriden, Conn • Mason, Ohio • Chicago

GALE
CENGAGE Learning·

Elizabeth Des Chenes, *Director, Content Strategy*
Cynthia Sanner, *Publisher*
Douglas Dentino, *Manager, New Product*

LIBRARY OF CONGRESS CATALOGING-IN-PUBLICATION DATA

Unemployment / Noël Merino, book editor.
      pages cm. -- (Global viewpoints)
      Summary: "Global Viewpoints: Unemployment: This title examines the topic around the issues of the global problem of unemployment, the victims of unemployment, the causes of unemployment, and the solutions to unemployment"--Provided by publisher.
      Includes bibliographical references and index.
      ISBN 978-0-7377-6916-6 (hardback) -- ISBN 978-0-7377-6917-3 (paperback)
      1. Unemployment--Juvenile literature. 2. Manpower policy--Juvenile literature.
      3. Unemployed--Juvenile literature. I. Merino, Noël, editor of compilation.
      HD5708.U574 2013
      331.13'7--dc23
                                                                    2013031433

Printed in the United States of America
    2 3 4 5 6   18 17 16 15 14

Contents

Chapter 3: The Causes of Unemployment

Population growth, inadequate and inappropriate education, employment regulations, and public sector employment have caused the problem of high youth unemployment.

Chapter 4: The Solutions to Unemployment

Foreword

"*The problems of all of humanity can
only be solved by all of humanity.*"
  —*Swiss author Friedrich Dürrenmatt*

Global interdependence has become an undeniable reality.
Mass media and technology have increased worldwide
access to information and created a society of global citizens.
Understanding and navigating this global community is a
challenge, requiring a high degree of information literacy and
a new level of learning sophistication.

Building on the success of its flagship series, Opposing
Viewpoints, Greenhaven Press has created the Global Viewpoints series to examine a broad range of current, often con-
troversial topics of worldwide importance from a variety of
international perspectives. Providing students and other readers with the information they need to explore global connec-
tions and think critically about worldwide implications, each
Global Viewpoints volume offers a panoramic view of a topic
of widespread significance.

Drugs, famine, immigration—a broad, international treat-
ment is essential to do justice to social, environmental, health,
and political issues such as these. Junior high, high school,
and early college students, as well as general readers, can all
use Global Viewpoints anthologies to discern the complexities
relating to each issue. Readers will be able to examine unique
national perspectives while, at the same time, appreciating the
interconnectedness that global priorities bring to all nations
and cultures.

Material in each volume is selected from a diverse range of
sources, including journals, magazines, newspapers, nonfiction
books, speeches, government documents, pamphlets, organiza-

11

tion newsletters, and position papers. Global Viewpoints is truly global, with material drawn primarily from international sources available in English and secondarily from US sources with extensive international coverage.

Features of each volume in the Global Viewpoints series include:

- An **annotated table of contents** that provides a brief summary of each essay in the volume, including the name of the country or area covered in the essay.

- An **introduction** specific to the volume topic.

- A **world map** to help readers locate the countries or areas covered in the essays.

- For each viewpoint, an **introduction** that contains notes about the author and source of the viewpoint explains why material from the specific country is being presented, summarizes the main points of the viewpoint, and offers three **guided reading questions** to aid in understanding and comprehension.

- **For further discussion** questions that promote critical thinking by asking the reader to compare and contrast aspects of the viewpoints or draw conclusions about perspectives and arguments.

- A worldwide list of **organizations to contact** for readers seeking additional information.

- A **periodical bibliography** for each chapter and a **bibliography of books** on the volume topic to aid in further research.

- A comprehensive **subject index** to offer access to people, places, events, and subjects cited in the text, with the countries covered in the viewpoints highlighted.

Global Viewpoints is designed for a broad spectrum of readers who want to learn more about current events, history, political science, government, international relations, economics, environmental science, world cultures, and sociology—students doing research for class assignments or debates, teachers and faculty seeking to supplement course materials, and others wanting to understand current issues better. By presenting how people in various countries perceive the root causes, current consequences, and proposed solutions to worldwide challenges, Global Viewpoints volumes offer readers opportunities to enhance their global awareness and their knowledge of cultures worldwide.

Introduction

"An uncertain economic outlook, and the inadequacy of policy to counter this, has weakened aggregate demand, holding back investment and hiring. This has prolonged the labour market slump in many countries, lowering job creation and increasing unemployment duration."

—*Guy Ryder,*
director-general of the International
Labour Organization (ILO)

Unemployment poses a problem for countries around the world. A country's labor force includes all those who are working as well as unemployed people who are looking for work. Those who are unemployed face economic hardship and drain public resources, where they are available. Thus, ensuring that all individuals in the labor force are able to work is in the best interest of individuals and communities. At any given time, a number of individuals will be unemployed due to the natural ebb and flow of employment between jobs or after finishing school—what economists call frictional unemployment—or from the seasonal nature of their work. However, when the fraction of the labor force that is unemployed becomes large and stagnant, there is cause for concern. Five years after the start of the global recession, countries around the world continue to struggle with elevated rates of stubborn unemployment.

In a recent report, "Global Employment Trends 2013," the International Labour Organization (ILO)—a specialized agency of the United Nations devoted to promoting social justice and internationally recognized human and labor rights—noted that although unemployment fell in 2010 and 2011, rising unemployment and lower growth in 2012 may be the start of a reversed trend. The ILO reports that four million people became unemployed in 2012, bringing the global unemployment total to 197.3 million people, up from 168.9 million in 2007, prior to the global recession.

The ILO notes that one million of those who became unemployed in 2012 were living in advanced economies, including North America, Europe, Australia, and New Zealand; the other three million who lost jobs that year were in developing economies, primarily in East Asia, South Asia, and sub-Saharan Africa. Nonetheless, the overall unemployment rates for 2012—the percentage of the job force without work—are still higher in advanced economies, with 8.6 percent of the workforce suffering from unemployment, compared to only 4.4 percent of workers in East Asia, 3.8 percent of the job force in South Asia, and 7.5 percent of workers in sub-Saharan Africa. Overall, the average unemployment rate for the world was approaching 6 percent in 2012, at 5.9 percent of the entire labor force. Latin American and the Caribbean stood just above the average at 6.6 percent. The region of Southeast Asia and the Pacific had the same rate as East Asia. The two regions topping the list with the highest unemployment rates in 2012 were North Africa, at 10.3 percent, and the Middle East, at 11.1 percent.

Youth unemployment in 2012 was higher than adult unemployment in every region of the world. Part of this is to be expected: Businesses are quicker to lay off new hires and inexperienced workers in times of economic downturn, and young people frequently experience some time of unemployment between the end of schooling and their first job. The global unemployment rate for youth in 2012 was 12.6 percent, slightly more than double the overall rate. The skewed youth unemployment rate stands out in a few areas where it is far more than double the overall rate: Youth in Southeast Asia and the

Pacific have an unemployment rate of 13 percent, and 28.1 percent of young people in the Middle East are unemployed.

Gender makes a difference to unemployment rates also. Whereas 7.9 percent of North African males are unemployed, 17.2 percent of females in North Africa are unemployed. Similarly, in the Middle East, women faced unemployment at a much higher rate than men in 2012, respectively 19.3 percent compared with 9.3 percent. Gender makes the opposite difference in East Asia, where 5.1 percent of males are unemployed compared with only 3.7 percent of females.

The ILO projects that unemployment will hit 6 percent in 2013 and stay at that level through 2017, with regional unemployment rates staying relatively stable. However, the ILO cautions that without internationally coordinated action to improve growth, stagnation in the job market and social turmoil could persist for years to come.

Though varying opinions exist on what level of unemployment is acceptable or normal, at a certain point all agree that a problem exists. The solution to the problem of unemployment, however, remains elusive. Controversy abounds on whether or not government should interfere with the market in attempting to create jobs. With respect to government assistance for the unemployed, strong opinions exist on both sides. On the one hand, some kind of safety net is said to help people transition from one job to the next, avoiding further social problems such as homelessness and crime. On the other hand, the safety net is sometimes charged with being a disincentive to work.

Unemployment rates vary widely around the world, but the unemployment rates in one region can have an impact elsewhere, as was seen by the impact of the global recession. Determining the best way to deal with unemployment worldwide is challenging because of the wide variety of conflicting opinions not only on what causes unemployment but also regarding the extent of the problem. Additionally, what works to alleviate unemployment in one part of the world may not be effective elsewhere. Shedding light on this ongoing debate, various viewpoints from around the world regarding the problem of unemployment, its causes, and its solutions are explored in *Global Viewpoints: Unemployment.*

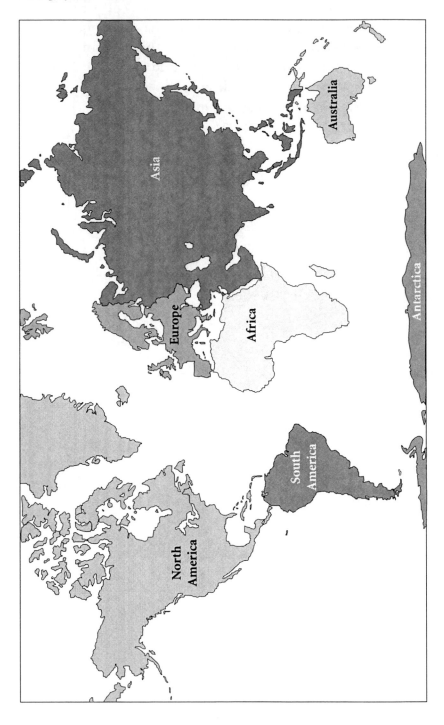

The Global Problem of Unemployment

Unemployment Is an Ongoing Feature of Economies Worldwide

Ceyda Öner

In the following viewpoint, published in Finance & Development *magazine by the International Monetary Fund (IMF), Ceyda Öner argues that the rate of unemployment is affected by economic activity, but that it does not respond immediately to either an increase or decrease in growth. However, Öner claims that no matter how much expansion an economy experiences, unemployment will never completely go away due to the inflexibility of wages and other factors, which cause the so-called natural rate of unemployment. Additionally, Öner cautions that not all people who are out of work or desiring more work are counted as unemployed by governments. Ceyda Öner is a Senior Economist in the IMF's Strategy, Policy, and Review Department.*

As you read, consider the following questions:

1. According to the author, what does it mean to say that unemployment is countercyclical?

2. Why doesn't the inflexibility of wages fully explain the perennial nature of unemployment, according to Öner?

3. According to Öner, what conditions must be met for a person to be considered unemployed for the purpose of government statistics?

A t the peak of the worldwide recession that began in 2008, the International Labour Office announced that global unemployment reached the highest level on record. More than 200 million people, 7 percent of the global workforce, were looking for jobs in 2009.

Unemployment and Economic Activity

It is not a coincidence that the global economy experienced the most severe case of unemployment during the worst economic crisis since the Great Depression. Unemployment is highly dependent on economic activity; in fact, growth and unemployment can be thought of as two sides of the same coin: When economic activity is high, more production happens overall, and more people are needed to produce the higher amount of goods and services. And when economic activity is low, firms reduce their workforce and unemployment rises. In that sense, unemployment is *countercyclical*, meaning it rises when economic growth is low and vice versa.

But unemployment does not fall in lockstep with an increase in growth. It is more common for businesses to first try to recover from a downturn by having the same number of employees do more work or turn out more products—that is, to increase their productivity. Only as the recovery takes hold are businesses likely to add workers. As a consequence, unemployment may start to come down only well after an economic recovery begins. The phenomenon works in reverse at the start of a downturn, when firms would rather reduce work hours, or impose some pay cuts before they let workers go.

Unemployment starts rising only when the downturn is prolonged. Because unemployment follows growth with a delay, it is considered a *lagging indicator* of economic activity.

Unemployment is highly dependent on economic activity.

How sensitive is the unemployment rate to economic growth? That depends on several factors, most notably on labor market conditions and regulations. One estimate of the strength of this relationship for the U.S. economy comes from Okun's law (named after the late U.S. economist Arthur Okun), which postulates that a decline in unemployment by 1 percentage point corresponds to a 3 percent rise in output. More recent estimates find that the consequent rise in output may be lower, possibly between 2 and 3 percent.

How far does this inverse relationship between growth and unemployment go? If economies kept expanding, would one expect to see unemployment disappear altogether? Actually this is not the case; even in the 2000s, when the global economy was prospering (at least until the crisis), global unemployment declined but never reached zero. This observation raises the question, why can unemployment never fall to zero?

The Perennial Nature of Unemployment

According to classical economic theory, every market, including the labor market, should have a point at which it clears—where supply and demand are equal. Yet the very existence of unemployment seems to imply that in labor markets around the world, the demand for and supply of labor fail to reach an equilibrium. Do labor markets continually fail?

Sometimes it is a matter of wages, or the unit price of labor, not adjusting to clear the market. Some workers, particularly skilled ones, may have *reservation wages* below which they are not willing to work, but which are higher than what employers are willing to pay. Alternatively, the wage an employer is willing to pay may be lower than the legal *minimum wage* set by governments to try to ensure that wages can sustain a living. When such rigidities in the labor market lead to a shortage of jobs, it creates *structural unemployment*, and those who are structurally unemployed tend to have longer spells of joblessness, on average.

Even in the 2000s, when the global economy was prospering (at least until the crisis), global unemployment declined but never reached zero.

But the inflexibility of wages does not fully explain the perennial nature of unemployment. Some level of unemployment will always exist for no other reason than that there always will be some people who are between jobs or just starting out their careers. These people are unemployed not because there is a shortage of jobs in the market, but because finding a job takes time. Such temporary spells of unemployment are referred to as *frictional unemployment*.

The Natural Rate of Unemployment

The combination of these factors brings about a long-term average around which the unemployment rate tends to fluctuate, called the *natural rate of unemployment* (NRU). The term "natural" does not mean it is a given that cannot be changed; to the contrary, it implies that labor market characteristics, which are mostly driven by policies, determine it. For example, the relatively high rate of unemployment in Europe compared with the United States is in part attributed to Europe's stronger unions and stricter labor regulations. These labor market institutions may give European workers a better bargaining position, but they can also render workers too expensive for employers. In the United States, unionization is

Jobs and Growth

In general, when real global gross domestic product is growing, the unemployment rate declines. The jobless rate generally increases when the world economy is shrinking.

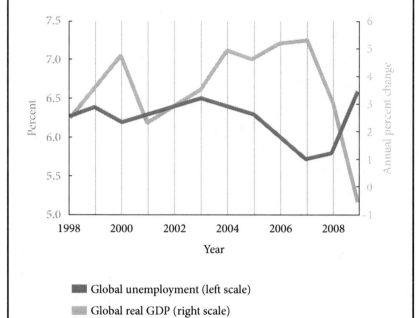

Global unemployment (left scale)
Global real GDP (right scale)

TAKEN FROM: Ceyda Öner, "Unemployment: The Curse of Joblessness," *Finance & Development*, updated March 28, 2012. www.imf.org.

lower and labor markets are more flexible, but workers have traditionally enjoyed higher employment rates than their European counterparts.

The natural rate of unemployment is sometimes called the *non-accelerating inflation rate of unemployment* (NAIRU), because it is consistent with an economy that is growing at its long-term potential, so there is no upward or downward pressure on inflation. The flip side of this argument suggests that whenever unemployment temporarily deviates from the NAIRU, inflation is affected. Consider a recession, a period of low economic activity. With lower demand for goods and services, firms start laying off workers and at the same time refrain from raising prices. So unemployment rises and inflation falls during recessions. This trade-off between unemployment and inflation—described by the Phillips curve (named after the late New Zealand economist William Phillips)—is only temporary, though; once prices adjust to a new equilibrium that clears the goods and services market, firms go back to producing at full capacity and unemployment once again falls—to the NAIRU.

Understanding what is behind the long-term equilibrium rate of unemployment helps policy makers understand how they can, and cannot, change it. For example, policies that try to lower unemployment by boosting consumer demand (thereby raising production) can do so only temporarily, and at the cost of higher inflation later. However, policies that are geared toward easing frictional or structural unemployment can boost employment without necessarily affecting inflation.

Understanding what is behind the long-term equilibrium rate of unemployment helps policy makers understand how they can, and cannot, change it.

But the NAIRU can also change over time without any explicit policy action: Structural changes such as technological advances and demographic shifts can have long-lasting effects on unemployment trends. For example, many economists agree that the technology boom of the 1990s increased labor productivity, making each worker more "desirable" to employers, and has therefore reduced the NAIRU—although there was an initial blip of unemployment as workers untrained in the technologies were displaced. A rapidly aging population—as is occurring in many advanced economies today—also contributes to fewer people in the job market and lower unemployment.

Measuring Unemployment

Not all people who don't work are unemployed. To be considered unemployed for government statistics, a person must not only be out of work, but also be actively looking for a job—for example, by sending out resumes. In the United States unemployment is measured by a monthly survey of households conducted for the Bureau of Labor Statistics and covers a representative sample of more than 100,000 individuals. The *labor force* includes both those with jobs and those looking for them. The *unemployment rate* is the percentage of the labor force that is looking for a job. The labor force is only a portion of the total population. The ratio of the labor force to the working-age population is called the *labor force participation rate*.

The labor force excludes people who are of working age but are neither employed nor looking for a job—such as students and homemakers. But the labor force also leaves out jobless people who were in the job market unsuccessfully for so long that they stopped looking for a job. Such *discouraged workers* are one reason why unemployment statistics can underestimate the true demand for jobs in an economy. Another form of *hidden unemployment* in statistics comes from counting as employed anyone who did *any* work for pay (or profit, if self-employed) in the week before the government survey. This hides the demand for work by people who would prefer full-time employment but cannot find it.

Global Unemployment Threatens to Cause a Renewed Recession Worldwide

United Nations

In the following viewpoint, the United Nations (UN) argues that weak economic growth worldwide is failing to replace jobs lost during the Great Recession. The UN claims the weak economies in Europe, the United States, and Japan are causing slow growth elsewhere. The UN contends that policy changes that reject austerity and support job creation are needed. The UN is an inter national organization of 193 member states committed to main-taining international peace and promoting better living standards and human rights.

As you read, consider the following questions:

1. According to the United Nations (UN), what was the unemployment rate in the euro zone in 2012?

2. What was the unemployment rate in the United States for most of 2012, according to the UN?

3. Improvements in economic conditions in what country are expected to boost economic growth in Latin America and the Caribbean in 2013, according to the UN?

Growth of the world economy has weakened considerably during 2012 and is expected to remain subdued in the coming two years, according to the United Nations [UN] in its latest issue of the "World Economic Situation and Prospects 2013" (WESP), published today [December 18, 2012]. The global economy is expected to grow at 2.4 per cent in 2013 and 3.2 per cent in 2014 a significant downgrade from the UN's forecast of half a year ago.

A Global Economic Slowdown

This pace of growth will be far from sufficient to overcome the continued jobs crisis that many countries are still facing. With existing policies and growth trends, it may take at least another five years for Europe and the United States to make up for the job losses caused by the Great Recession of 2008–2009.

Weaknesses in the major developed economies are at the root of the global economic slowdown. The WESP report stresses that most of them, but particularly those in Europe, are trapped in a vicious cycle of high unemployment, financial-sector fragility, heightened sovereign risks, fiscal austerity and low growth. Several European economies and the euro zone as a whole are already in recession, and euro zone unemployment increased further to a record high of almost 12 per cent this year. Also, the US economy slowed significantly during 2012 and growth is expected to remain meager at 1.7 per cent in 2013. Deflationary conditions continue to prevail in Japan.

The economic woes in Europe, Japan and the United States are spilling over to developing countries through weaker demand for their exports and heightened volatility in capital flows and commodity prices. The larger developing economies also face homegrown problems, however, with some (including China) facing much weakened investment demand because of financing constraints in some sectors of the economy and excess production capacity elsewhere. Most low-income countries have held up relatively well so far, but are now also facing intensified adverse spillover effects from the slowdown in both developed and major middle-income countries.

Weaknesses in the major developed economies are at the root of the global economic slowdown.

The prospects for the next two years continue to be challenging, fraught with major uncertainties and risks slanted towards the downside. Rob Vos, the UN's team leader for the report, warned: "A worsening of the euro area crisis, the 'fiscal cliff' in the United States and a hard landing in China could cause a new global recession. Each of these risks could cause global output losses of between 1 and 3 per cent."

The Need for Policy Changes

The UN report further assesses that present policy stances fall short of what is needed to spur economic recovery and address the jobs crisis. While policy efforts have been significant, especially in the euro zone, in trying to redress sovereign debt distress, the combination of fiscal austerity and expansionary monetary policies has had mixed success so far in calming financial markets and even less so in strengthening economic growth and job creation.

It is essential to change course in fiscal policy, the UN report says, and shift the focus from short-term consolidation to robust economic growth with medium- to long-term fiscal sustainability. Premature fiscal austerity should be avoided and, while necessary, fiscal consolidation should focus on medium-term, rather than short-term adjustment.

The report stresses that the reorientation of fiscal policies should be internationally coordinated and aligned with structural policies that support direct job creation and green growth. It further recommends that monetary policies be better coordinated internationally and regulatory reforms of financial sectors be accelerated in order to stem exchange rate and capital flow volatility, which pose risks to the economic prospects of developing countries. There is also a need to secure sufficient development assistance to help the poorest nations accelerate progress towards poverty reduction goals and invest in sustainable development.

Observing that development aid is declining, the UN report notes that fiscal austerity in donor countries is not only detrimental to their own economic recovery, but certainly should not come at the expense of the development efforts of the poorest nations.

Economic Recession in Europe

Several European economies are already in recession. In Germany, growth has slowed significantly, while France's economy is stagnating. A number of new policy initiatives have been taken by the euro area authorities in 2012, including the Outright Monetary Transactions (OMT) programme and steps towards greater fiscal integration and coordinated financial supervision and regulation, but there has been no significant initiative towards boosting growth in the short run or tackling the ever-mounting crisis in the labour markets.

In the United Nations baseline forecast, the euro area economy is expected to grow by only 0.3 per cent in 2013 and 1.4 per cent in 2014, a feeble recovery from the 0.5 per cent decline in 2012. Because of the dynamics of the vicious circle, the risk for a much worse scenario remains high and could be triggered by deeper fiscal cuts and delayed implementation of the OMT programme.

The unemployment rate continued to climb to a record high in the euro area during 2012, up by more than one percentage point from one year ago. Conditions are worse in Spain and Greece, where more than a quarter of the working population is without a job and more than half of the youth

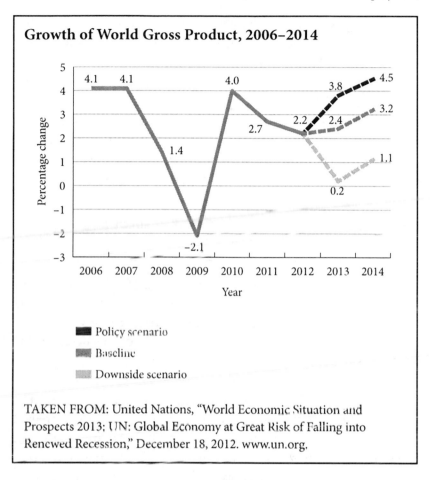

Growth of World Gross Product, 2006–2014

TAKEN FROM: United Nations, "World Economic Situation and Prospects 2013; UN: Global Economy at Great Risk of Falling into Renewed Recession," December 18, 2012. www.un.org.

is unemployed. Only a few economies in the region, such as Austria, Germany, Luxembourg and the Netherlands, register low unemployment rates of about 5 per cent. Unemployment rates in Central and Eastern Europe also edged up slightly in 2012, resulting from fiscal austerity and the economic slowdown in the euro area.

A Weak US Economy

The United States economy weakened notably during 2012, and growth prospects for 2013 and 2014 remain sluggish. On the upside, the beleaguered housing sector is showing some nascent signs of recovery, and further support is expected from the new round of quantitative easing recently launched by the Federal Reserve (Fed).

The unemployment rate stayed above 8 per cent for the most part of 2012, but dropped to just below that level from September onwards. However, the labour participation rate is at a record low, while the shares of long-term unemployment reached historic highs of 40.6 per cent (jobless for 6 months or longer) and 31.4 per cent (one year or longer).

The unemployment rate continued to climb to a record high in the euro area during 2012.

The WESP report says that the lingering uncertainties about the fiscal stance continue to hold back business investment. External demand is also expected to remain weak. In the baseline outlook, growth of GDP (gross domestic product) in the United States is forecast to decelerate to 1.7 per cent in 2013 from an already anaemic pace of 2.1 per cent in 2012. Risks remain high for a much bleaker scenario, emanating from the "fiscal cliff," which would entail a drop in aggregate demand by as much as 4 per cent of GDP during 2013 and 2014, as well as from the spillover effects of a further intensification of the euro area crisis and a possible hard landing of the Chinese economy and further weakening of other major developing economies.

Weakened Economies in Asia

Japan's GDP is forecast to grow at 0.6 per cent in 2013 and 0.8 per cent in 2014, down from 1.5 per cent in 2012. Economic growth in Japan in 2012 was up from a year ago, mainly driven by the reconstruction work and recovery from the earthquake-related disasters of 2011. The Japanese government took additional measures to stimulate private consumption. Exports faced strong headwinds from the slowdown in global demand and appreciation of the yen.

According to the WESP report, Japan's economy is expected to slow as a result of the phasing out of incentives to private consumption and a new measure that increases the tax on consumption, reduces pension benefits and cuts government spending.

Economies in developing Asia have weakened considerably during 2012, the UN report states, as the region's growth engines, China and India, have shifted into lower gear. While a significant deceleration in exports has been a key factor behind the slowdown, both economies also face a number of structural challenges that hamper growth. Given persistent inflationary pressures and large fiscal deficits, the scope for policy stimulus in India and other South Asian countries is limited. China and many East Asian economies, in contrast, possess much greater space for countercyclical policy. In the outlook, average growth in East Asia is forecast to pick up mildly to 6.2 per cent in 2013, from the estimated 5.8 per cent in 2012. GDP growth in South Asia is expected to average 5.0 per cent in 2013, up from 4.4 per cent in 2012, led by a moderate recovery of India's economy.

Economies in developing Asia have weakened considerably during 2012.

Slower Growth Elsewhere

Economies in Africa are forecast to see a slight moderation in output growth in 2013 to 4.8 per cent, down from 5.0 per cent in 2012, according to the WESP report. Major factors underpinning this continued growth trajectory include the strong performance of oil-exporting countries, continued fiscal spending on infrastructure projects, and expanding economic ties with Asian economies. However, Africa remains plagued by numerous challenges, including armed conflicts in various parts of the region. Growth of income per capita will continue, but at a pace considered insufficient to accelerate poverty reduction.

Contrasting trends are found in Western Asia, according to the UN report. Most oil-exporting countries have experienced robust growth supported by record-high oil revenues and government spending. Social unrest and political instability, notably in the Syrian Arab Republic, continue to elevate the risk assessment for the entire region. On average, GDP growth in the region is expected to decelerate to 3.3 per cent in 2012 and 2013, from 6.7 per cent in 2011.

The UN report indicates that GDP growth in Latin America and the Caribbean decelerated notably during 2012, led by weaker export demand and lower prices of non-food commodities in the region's exports. In the outlook, subject to the risks of a further downturn, the baseline projection is for a return to moderate economic growth rates, led by expected improvements in economic conditions in Brazil. For the region as a whole, GDP growth is forecast to average 3.9 per cent in the baseline for 2013, compared with 3.2 per cent in 2012.

Economic growth in the Russian Federation and other countries of the Commonwealth of Independent States (CIS) was robust in 2012, although it moderated in the second half of the year. Firm commodity prices, especially the prices of oil and natural gas, held up growth among energy-exporting economies, including the Russian Federation and Kazakhstan. In the outlook, GDP for the CIS is expected to grow by 3.8 per cent in 2013, the same as in 2012.

Unemployment in the European Union Varies Among Member States

Eurostat

In the following viewpoint, Eurostat contends that unemployment in the European Union at the start of 2013 had increased from the previous year to 11.9 percent, although rates in individual countries ranged from 4.9 percent to 27 percent. Eurostat notes that the unemployment rates for youth are particularly high, and rates for women are slightly higher than for men. Eurostat claims long-term unemployment is an issue for policy makers to address and suggests that education protects against unemployment. Eurostat is the statistical office of the European Union and is based in Luxembourg.

As you read, consider the following questions:

1. According to Eurostat, which European Union country had the lowest unemployment rate in January 2013?

2. What were the unemployment rates for women and men in the European Union in 2011, according to the author?

3. According to Eurostat, in 2011 what percentage of the workforce in Europe had been unemployed for more than a year?

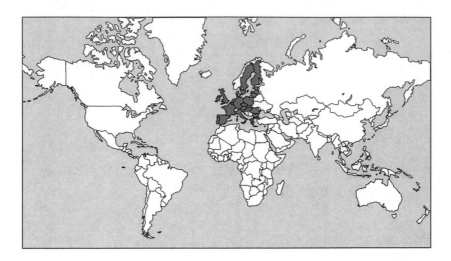

Eurostat estimates that 26,217 million men and women in the EU-27 [twenty-seven countries of the European Union], of whom 18,998 million were in the euro area (EA-17), were unemployed in January 2013. Compared with December 2012, the number of persons unemployed increased by 222,000 in the EU-27 and by 201,000 in the euro area. Compared with January 2012, unemployment rose by 1,890,000 in the EU-27 and by 1,909,000 in the euro area.

Unemployment in Europe

The euro area seasonally adjusted unemployment rate was 11.9% in January 2013, up from 11.8% in December 2012; it was 10.8% in January 2012. The EU-27 unemployment rate was 10.8% in January 2013, up from 10.7% in the previous month; it was 10.1% in January 2012.

Among the member states, the lowest unemployment rates were recorded in Austria (4.9%), Germany and Luxembourg (both 5.3%) and the Netherlands (6.0%), and the highest rates in Greece (27.0% in November 2012), Spain (26.2%) and Portugal (17.6%).

Compared with a year ago, the unemployment rate increased in nineteen member states, fell in seven and remained stable in Denmark. The largest decreases were observed in Estonia (11.1% to 9.9% between December 2011 and December 2012), Latvia (15.5% to 14.4% between the fourth quarters of 2011 and 2012), Romania (7.4% to 6.6%) and the United Kingdom (8.3% to 7.7% between November 2011 and November 2012). The highest increases were registered in Greece (20.8% to 27.0% between November 2011 and November 2012), Cyprus (9.9% to 14.7%), Portugal (14.7% to 17.6%) and Spain (23.6% to 26.2%).

Between January 2012 and January 2013, the unemployment rate for males increased from 10.6% to 11.8% in the euro area and from 10.0% to 10.8% in the EU-27. The female unemployment rate increased from 11.0% to 12.1% in the euro area and from 10.2% to 10.9% in the EU-27.

In January 2013, 5,732 million young people (under 25) were unemployed in the EU-27, of whom 3,642 million were in the euro area. Compared with January 2012, youth unemployment increased by 264,000 in the EU-27 and by 295,000 in the euro area. In January 2013, the youth unemployment rate was 23.6% in the EU-27 and 24.2% in the euro area. In January 2012 it was 22.4% and 21.9% respectively. In January 2013 the lowest rates were observed in Germany (7.9%), Austria (9.9%) and the Netherlands (10.3%), and the highest in Greece (59.4% in November 2012), Spain (55.5%) and Italy (38.7%).

Compared with a year ago, the unemployment rate increased in nineteen member states, fell in seven and remained stable in Denmark.

In January 2013, the unemployment rate in the USA was 7.9%. In Japan it was 4.2% in December 2012.

Unemployment Trends, 2000–2011

In early 2000, just less than 20 million persons were unemployed in the EU-27, slightly below 9% of the total labour force. This figure fell to around 19 million (or 8.5%) in early

2001 before rising back to around 21 million persons by the middle of 2002, where it remained until the middle of 2005. From mid-2005 there was a period of several years of steadily declining unemployment within the EU-27. By the first quarter of 2008, EU-27 unemployment hit a low of 16 million persons (equivalent to a rate of 6.7%) before rising sharply in the wake of the economic crisis. In 2010 and 2011, the average unemployment rate in the EU-27 was 9.7%, the highest annual rates recorded since the start of the series in 2000.

The unemployment rate in the euro area (EA-17) followed roughly the same trend as in the EU-27. However, between 2000 and the middle of 2004 the unemployment rate in the euro area was below that recorded in the EU-27. This pattern was subsequently reversed as unemployment declined more rapidly in the member states which do not yet have the euro between 2005 and 2008. During the economic crisis, unemployment increased at a considerable pace, as in the EU-27. While in the EU-27 the growth in unemployment slowed down in 2011, the average unemployment rate for the EA-17 hit 10.2%, the highest rate since 1999.

In 2000, the unemployment rate in the United States was around 4%, considerably lower than in the EU. It remained much lower until early 2008, when unemployment started to increase rapidly. By mid-2009, the unemployment rate in the United States had reached the same level as in the EU, and the annual average rate in 2009 was higher in the US than in the EU-27. In 2010 and 2011, annual average unemployment rates in the US, while still comparatively high, dropped again below EU-27 levels. Unemployment rates in Japan were much lower than in the EU, and this was the case without exception throughout the last ten years for which data are available.

Unemployment by Age and Gender

Youth unemployment rates are generally much higher than unemployment rates for all ages. High youth unemployment rates do reflect the difficulties faced by young people in finding jobs. However, this does not necessarily mean that the group of unemployed persons aged between 15 and 24 is large because many young people are studying full-time and are therefore neither working nor looking for a job (so they are not part of the labour force which is used as the denominator for calculating the unemployment rate). For this reason, youth unemployment ratios are calculated as well, according to a somewhat different concept: the unemployment ratio calculates the share of unemployed for the whole population. . . . Youth unemployment ratios in the EU are much lower than youth unemployment rates; they have however also risen since 2008 due to the effects of the recent crisis on the labour market.

The youth unemployment rate in the EU-27 was around twice as high as the rate for the total population throughout the last decade. The EU-27 youth unemployment rate was systematically higher than in the euro area between 2000 and early 2008; since this date, these two rates were very close, until mid-2010, when the EU-27 youth unemployment rate started to increase more strongly than that of the EA-17. While youth unemployment thus increased in both areas during the crisis, the increase has been more relevant for the EU-27, despite the lower overall unemployment rate in that area.

Historically, women have been more affected by unemployment than men. In 2000, the unemployment rate for women in the EU-27 was around 10%, while the rate for men was around 8%. By the end of 2002, this gender gap had narrowed to around 1.3 percentage points and between 2002 and early 2007 this gap remained more or less constant. In recent years, most markedly since the first quarter of 2008, male and female unemployment rates in the EU-27 have converged and by the second quarter of 2009 the male unemployment rate was higher. The annual average unemployment rates for 2009 and 2010 were consequently slightly higher for men (9.1%

and 9.7% respectively) than for women (9.0% and 9.6%); in 2011 however, unemployment for males slightly declined in the EU-27, while that of women continued to increase such that the rate for males was again lower at 9.6% than that for females (9.8%).

The youth unemployment rate in the EU-27 was around twice as high as the rate for the total population throughout the last decade.

A Concern About Long-Term Unemployment

The overall unemployment rate in the EU-27 reached 9.7% in 2011, thus staying stable at a high level in comparison with 2010. The impact of the economic crisis on unemployment in the years from 2008 to 2010 has completely wiped out the reduction experienced in the unemployment rate between 2004 and 2008. In the United States, where the unemployment rate grew from 9.3% to 9.6% between 2009 and 2010, it dropped again in 2011 to 8.9%. Between 2008 and 2009, the unemployment rate had increased by a staggering 3.5 percentage points.

The unemployment rate rose in 12 member states between 2010 and 2011, dropped in 13 and remained stable in two, France and Italy. The highest decreases in the annual average unemployment rates between 2010 and 2011 were experienced in the Baltic countries, with Estonia in the lead (-4.4 ppt) followed by Latvia (-3.3 ppt) and Lithuania (-2.4 ppt). The unemployment rate also fell in Belgium, the Czech Republic, Germany, Hungary, Malta, the Netherlands, Austria, Slovakia, Finland and Sweden. The highest increases were reported in Greece (+5.1 ppt), Portugal (+1.9 ppt), Spain (+1.6 ppt), Cyprus (+1.3 ppt) and Bulgaria (+1.0 ppt). Increases below one percentage point were reported in Denmark, Ireland, Luxembourg, Poland, Romania, Slovenia and the UK. For the fourth year in a row, Spain remained the country with the highest overall unemployment rate in 2011, at 21.7%. The dispersion of unemployment across the EU-27 continued to increase during 2011.

Long-term unemployment is one of the main concerns of policy makers. Apart from its financial and social effects on personal life, long-term unemployment negatively affects social cohesion and, ultimately, may hinder economic growth. In total, 4.1% of the labour force in the EU-27 in 2011 had been unemployed for more than one year; more than half of these, 2.2% of the labour force, had been unemployed for more than two years.

Educational qualifications are still the best insurance against unemployment, which clearly increases the lower the level of education attained.

The Best Insurance Against Unemployment

For the first time since the calculation of EU-27 unemployment statistics started (in 2000), the unemployment rate for women was lower than that for men in 2009, and remained so in 2010. In 2011, this effect had reversed again, showing female unemployment rates at 9.8% against 9.6% for males. In the euro area, the gap was even higher, with female unemployment at 10.5% and male unemployment at 9.9%. Male unemployment rates were higher than the corresponding rates for women during 2011 in 12 out of 27 member states. The gap between male and female unemployment rates varied from -6.3 percentage points in Greece to +6.9 percentage points in Ireland.

The youth unemployment rate in the EU-27 was more than double the overall unemployment rate in 2011. At 21.4%, more than one out of every five young persons in the labour force was not employed, but looking and available for a job. In the euro area, the youth unemployment rate was marginally lower at 20.8%. The unemployment rate among young persons was higher than the rate among those aged between 25 and 74 in all of the member states. In Spain (46.4%), Greece (44.4%), Slovakia (33.2%), Lithuania (32.9%), and Portugal (30.1%) youth unemployment rates were particularly high. The Netherlands (7.6%), Austria (8.3%), and Germany (8.6%) were the only member states with a youth unemployment rate below 10%.

Educational qualifications are still the best insurance against unemployment, which clearly increases the lower the level of education attained. This characteristic was noted in all member states except for Greece and Cyprus in 2011, as the average unemployment rate in the EU-27 for those having attained at most a lower secondary education was 16.7%, much higher than the rate of unemployment for those that had obtained a tertiary education qualification (5.6%).

Long-Term Unemployment Is a Serious Problem in the United States

Gary Burtless

In the following viewpoint, Gary Burtless argues that long-term unemployment has increased since the Great Recession and that political indifference is making a solution challenging. Burtless claims that the longer a worker is unemployed, the less chance there is of him obtaining a job. Burtless contends that the United States is not generous to the unemployed with unemployment benefits, compared to European countries. Burtless concludes that long-term unemployment is a serious concern that needs to be addressed. Burtless holds the John C. and Nancy D. Whitehead Chair in Economic Studies at the Brookings Institution.

As you read, consider the following questions:

1. According to Burtless, from 2007 to 2011 the percentage of the nation's unemployed who had been jobless for longer than six months increased by how much?

2. What percentage of unemployed Americans collected unemployment insurance in early 2010, at the peak of stimulus spending, according to the author?

Gary Burtless, "Long-Term Unemployment: Anatomy of the Scourge," *Milken Institute Review*, vol. 14, no. 3, Third Quarter 2012, pp. 54–57, 59–61. Copyright © 2012 by Milken Institute. All rights reserved. Reproduced by permission.

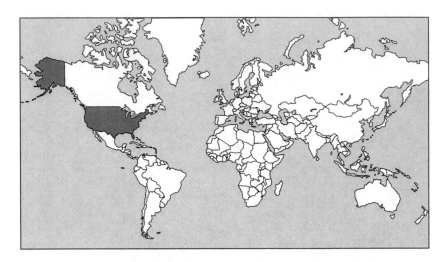

3. According to Burtless, from October 2008 to September 2009 the monthly probability of losing one's job was what percentage?

The U.S. Bureau of Labor Statistics [BLS] defines an unemployed person as a potential worker who is currently jobless, has actively sought work in the previous four weeks and is available for work. The BLS also counts workers as unemployed who have been temporarily laid off and anticipate being recalled, even if they're not actively looking for another job. People who are neither employed nor unemployed by this definition are classified as "not in the labor force."

The Long-Term Unemployed

The government does not have an official definition of "long term" unemployment; economists generally use six months or a year of involuntary joblessness as the benchmark. Because unemployment lasting more than a year has historically been rare in the United States, in many BLS reports the chronically unemployed are simply placed in the "27 weeks or longer" category.

In other industrialized countries, by contrast, the long-term unemployed have long represented a large fraction of total unemployment. In 2007, for example, more than a fifth of France's unemployed and almost 40 percent of Germany's had been out of work for two years or longer. (That same year, fewer than 18 percent of unemployed Americans reported being jobless longer than 6 months, and fewer than one in 10 had been unemployed for as much as a year.)

Very long periods of unemployment were only rarely reported in the United States before the Great Recession. Laid-off workers, along with those just entering the labor force, typically found jobs relatively quickly. From 1990 to 2007, for example, more than a quarter of all American workers who were classified as unemployed in a given month found jobs the following month.

The pace of exit from unemployment is sensitive to the business cycle—finding a job is, of course, easier in a boom than in a bust. At the end of the prosperous 1990s, more than one-third of the unemployed in a given month had found work one month later. Job-finding success fell sharply in the 2001 recession, reaching a low point in early 2003 before recovering during the economic expansion that ended in 2007. The 2008–9 recession brought another plunge in the rate of worker exit from unemployment. The monthly job-finding rate of the unemployed was 28 percent in 2007; by the second half of 2009 it had fallen to just 16 percent. That is, at the nadir of the recession, less than one in six unemployed workers was successful in finding a job within a month.

The Challenge for Jobless Workers

Though jobless workers were less successful in finding jobs in the 2008–9 recession, they were also less likely to give up their search by dropping out of the workforce altogether. The predictable result: average unemployment durations lengthened. Even though the job-finding rate slowly improved after the worst of the recession passed, at the beginning of 2012 it was still one-third lower than the average between 1990 and 2007.

The obvious reason jobless workers were less successful in finding jobs after 2007 is that employers had fewer vacancies to fill: The job-opening rate fell more than 40 percent from 2007 to 2009. The vacancy rate has grown since the recession ended, but in early 2012 it was still almost one-fifth below the 2007 level. In the last quarter of 2007, there were 1.6 unemployed workers for every job vacancy reported by the BLS. Two years later, this ratio had jumped to six to one. And while the ratio improved during the recovery, it was still 3.8 to one at the end of 2011.

Very long periods of unemployment were only rarely reported in the United States before the Great Recession.

A worker's success at finding a job tends to decline with the length of unemployment. The percentage of all unemployed who found work within a month fell from 28 percent in 2007 to 17 percent in 2011. But in both years, workers were much more successful finding jobs in the first weeks of joblessness. In 2007, for example, workers who had been unemployed less than 5 weeks had a 37 percent chance of landing a job within a month. Workers reporting unemployment longer than six months had only a 16 percent chance of finding employment in the coming month.

The Great Recession has thus pushed jobless workers into unemployment-duration groups with poor odds of finding work, even after economic recovery. From 2007 to 2011, the fraction of the nation's unemployed who were unemployed six months or longer increased from 18 percent to 44 percent...

The Economics of Unemployment Benefits

Even in serious recessions, jobless Americans tend to be out of work for shorter periods than their European counterparts. This difference became evident in the 1980s, when for the first time in decades, European unemployment rose above the U.S.

rate and remained there. A popular explanation was the difference in social protection on the two sides of the Atlantic. By generously insuring laid-off workers against earnings losses for very long periods, the argument goes, European countries reduced unemployed workers' incentive to search intensively for jobs. The United States provided less generous protection, especially for workers who remained jobless for very long.

So why didn't these differences in social protection have a similar impact before the 1980s? One possibility is that before the big recessions in the mid-1970s and early 1980s relatively few European workers were exposed to the adverse incentives created by generous jobless benefits. And even those who were exposed didn't have much time to develop a taste for living on the dole. Indeed, labor markets were so tight that many rich Western European countries were forced to import labor to make up for the shortfall of native workers.

Though unemployment insurance [UI] and other income protection programs have been scaled back in Europe, Europeans are still better sheltered than Americans. According to the OECD [Organisation for Economic Co-operation and Development], the United States ranks near the bottom in generosity among affluent nations when income replacement rates were measured over a two-year unemployment spell. In 2007, just 14 percent of an American worker's pre-layoff earnings were replaced. The median net replacement rate among the other 20 countries surveyed was 60 percent.

The Special Stimulus Measures

The special stimulus measures passed in 2008 and 2009 did narrow the gap. The two-year replacement rate increased from 14 percent to 43 percent, mainly because workers were permitted to collect unemployment insurance benefits for greatly extended periods. By late fall of 2009, workers in most states with high unemployment rates could draw up to 99 weeks of benefits—almost four times longer than in 2007.

In addition to extending UI protection, the stimulus programs temporarily increased weekly payments, reduced income-tax liability on unemployment benefits, and provided generous subsidies for laid-off workers who chose to keep on buying health insurance through their ex-employers. Weekly benefits are now back to pre-recession levels, and the extensions of eligibility for benefits are slated to expire at the end of the year [2012]. But even if Congress once again extends the extensions, it will almost certainly let them lapse when unemployment dips below 7 percent.

Though unemployment insurance and other income protection programs have been scaled back in Europe, Europeans are still better sheltered than Americans.

More generally, there is no reason to believe that the country is becoming more generous to the unemployed. The percentage of unemployed eligible for UI programs fell substantially in the 1980s and has only partially recovered since then. At the peak of stimulus spending in early 2010, nearly 70 percent of unemployed Americans collected UI—a higher percentage than in the recessions of the last few decades, but a smaller percentage than in 1975. . . .

The Consequences of Chronic Unemployment

There are good reasons to worry about long-term unemployment. The main focus of concern is, of course, the welfare of those unemployed. The costs exacted by a recession are distributed unevenly, with the long-term unemployed suffering the most. UI provides very modest compensation for the income losses they experience.

Economists also worry about the enduring consequences of permitting unemployment to become chronic. Some of those affected eventually exit the workforce, retiring long before their capacity and willingness to work end. Others may find employment, but in jobs that are a poor match for their skills and experience. These losses have consequences for the broader economy, shrinking potential output and increasing the burden on costly transfer programs, including Medicaid and Social Security Disability Insurance.

There are good reasons to worry about long-term unemployment.

A secondary consequence is that the long-term unemployed eventually become invisible to both the labor market and to policy makers, and thus cease to serve as a check on wage inflation as the economy nears full capacity. High unemployment leads workers to be more cautious in their wage demands and makes employers more reluctant to grant big pay increases. It's unclear, though, whether the long-term unemployed have the same weight as the short-term unemployed in changing labor market expectations.

The Impact on Wages and Prices

The short- and long-term unemployed would have equal weight if employers regarded them as equally eligible to fill job vacancies. If they don't view the long-term unemployed as adequate substitutes for newly laid-off workers, however, an increase in the long-term unemployment rate should have a smaller restraining influence on wages and prices than an equivalent increase in short-term unemployment.

Ricardo Llaudes, an economist at the European Central Bank, investigated the relative impact of short- and long-term unemployment rate, examining the experiences of 19 rich countries between the late 1960s and 2002. In most of them, the short-term unemployed exerted a considerably greater restraining influence than their long-term counterparts. In France, for example, their estimated impact was three times as great.

The difference was much less pronounced in the United States, where short-term unemployment has only a 16 percent greater weight than the long-term unemployment. Llaudes's data do not, however, include the big run-up in long-term unemployment since 2007. And conceivably, the American experience is converging with the European, a process that effectively raises the "natural" rate of unemployment—the lowest rate sustainable without inflation.

The Danger of Political Indifference

From a political perspective, familiarity with long-term unemployment may breed collective indifference; addressing the challenge of long-term unemployment becomes a lower priority for policy makers when the media (and voters) lose interest. If each American worker faced identical odds of losing a job, and each job loser then suffered an identical spell of unemployment, most workers would probably take keen interest in minimizing both the risk of unemployment and its likely duration. In fact, the risk of losing a job varies tremendously across regions, industries and job categories, and the duration of unemployment varies greatly among those who do lose their jobs. As a result, the risk of job loss is of little concern to many workers (especially when the economy is growing) and the severe problems of the long-term unemployed become a smaller concern.

The percentage of employed workers who became unemployed in a typical month averaged about 1.2 percent in 2007, the last year of the economic expansion. From October 2008 to September 2009, the monthly probability of losing one's job surged to 1.8 percent. Most workers became acutely aware of the increased risk, providing policy makers with a base of support for measures to halt the economic slide and to aid the workers harmed by it.

But the monthly percentage of workers who become unemployed has fallen since the economy began to expand in late 2009. Though job-loss rates remain higher than they were at the end of the last expansion, they are well below their recession peaks. Rousing sympathy for the unemployed in general, and the long-term unemployed in particular, is thus becoming more difficult.

Unemployment in Africa Is Widespread, Especially Among the Young

Jonathan Oppenheimer and Michael Spicer

In the following viewpoint, Jonathan Oppenheimer and Michael Spicer argue that there is a crisis of joblessness and informal employment throughout Africa, especially in sub-Saharan urban centers. The authors claim that despite economic growth, there has not been the needed increase in formal jobs, especially for young people. Oppenheimer and Spicer conclude that there is a potential for positive change if formal sector employment can be increased. Oppenheimer is founder of the Brenthurst Foundation in South Africa; Spicer is vice president at Business Leadership South Africa.

As you read, consider the following questions:

1. What seven African megacities do the authors identify?
2. According to the authors, what is the unemployment rate among fifteen- to twenty-four-year-old South Africans?
3. What is the primary school completion rate across sub-Saharan Africa, according to the authors?

Jonathan Oppenheimer and Michael Spicer, "Creating Employment in Africa," *Putting Young Africans to Work: Addressing Africa's Youth Unemployment Crisis*, Brenthurst Foundation, September 2011, pp. 14–17. Copyright © 2011 by The Brenthurst Foundation. All rights reserved. Reproduced by permission.

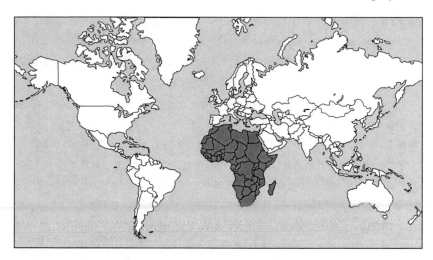

Youth (un)employment is one of the greatest drivers shaping African politics over the next generation.

The Urbanisation of Africa

Sub-Saharan Africa's population is predicted to increase from 800 million today to 1.5 billion within a generation. Pressure on finite resources (notably water) and on regimes, institutions and governments will increase.

The continent will, by 2025, be an urban continent. One hundred years ago just 5 per cent of Africans lived in cities. Today it is around 40 per cent. In 2025 it will be over 50 per cent. This goes hand in hand with the elevation of a number of African cities to the megacity bracket. In 1963 Lagos had just 665,000 inhabitants. It is expected to become the world's 11th biggest city by 2015 with 16 million inhabitants. Africa's other megacities are Cairo (Egypt), Accra (Ghana), Johannesburg-Pretoria (South Africa), Khartoum (Sudan), Kinshasa-Brazzaville (Democratic Republic of the Congo and Republic of the Congo), and Nairobi (Kenya).

By 2025, nearly one-quarter of the world's young people (under the age of 25) will be from sub-Saharan Africa—an extraordinary statistic. And many of them will be living in

Africa's cities. With an urbanisation rate, in some African countries, as high as (or over) 10 per cent per annum, keeping ahead of the need for jobs for new entrants demands annual economic growth rates close to 20 per cent annually.

Despite much better performance, as a result of the slow growth over the 50 years of independence, the majority of urban dwellers in sub-Saharan Africa live in slums, [according to Stephanie Hanson of the Council on Foreign Relations] 'without durable housing or legal rights to their land. At least one-quarter of African city dwellers do not have access to electricity.' Under half have access to piped water, while waste disposal is often rudimentary at best. In Kibera, Nairobi's largest slum housing perhaps as many as one million people, plastic bags are used as 'flying toilets'. At the same time, an estimated 60 per cent of urban employment is estimated to be in the informal sector, limiting tax revenues and, for entrepreneurs, access to financing and markets.

Unemployment in Africa

Joblessness is endemic in Africa, especially among the young. Youth unemployment and underemployment in some countries is as high as 80 per cent, including relatively well-performing states such as Mozambique and Ghana. To provide another example, Zambia had three million people at independence. Today it has 13 million. But whereas there were 300,000 formal sector jobs at independence in 1964, today there are under 500,000, excluding public sector workers. And most of the three million or so young people are unemployed. No wonder politics is often fraught and people are angry in spite of a recent record of consistent growth in Africa.

The problem is acute in post-conflict countries. Historically, not only do nearly half of such states slide back to conflict within ten years, but their period of recovery from war is typically at least as long as the period of decline. This unfortunate axiom is of particular relevance to Africa and to some of its most important and largest countries, including the DR [Democratic Republic of the] Congo, Angola and Sudan/South Sudan. Young people in post-conflict countries are especially susceptible to extremism and militancy when there are few or no meaningful livelihood options.

Joblessness is endemic in Africa, especially among the young.

Although many countries in Africa have enjoyed unprecedented economic growth over the past decade, this has not translated into formal jobs. Government has found it difficult to bridge the gap between growth and jobs. There are a number of reasons for this, foremost among them being the lack of competitiveness and productivity when compared to South and East Asia and China; the relatively small number employed directly by the natural resource sector, which has driven the boom times and provided a fiscal boost in the process; weak and expensive infrastructure; and a lack of suitable skills. Hence the question often asked today throughout the continent: What can we produce that China cannot make cheaper than us?

The Need to Increase Formal Sector Employment

Some countries, notably South Africa, have failed to increase formal sector employment much, if at all, largely because labour laws have made employment less attractive for employers. Wage rates escalating way ahead of productivity, the cost of hiring and firing, and a generally inflexible labour market have strengthened existing trends to capital intensity and outsourcing by employers. This has taken place against a global trend to more temporary employment as workplaces change fundamentally. The South African treasury notes that just 13.1 million South Africans are employed: 'two out of five persons

Challenges in Africa

Africa has strengthened the recovery that started after the global financial and economic crisis, with GDP [gross domestic product] growth rising from 2.3 per cent in 2009 to 4.7 per cent in 2010. For the continent as a whole, per capita GDP also grew in 2010, by 2.4 per cent. Growth prospects remain optimistic (despite downside risks), and Africa is looking forward to growth of 5 per cent in 2011. . . .

Africa's unemployment remains high, however, and its economic rebound is yet to translate into meaningful reductions in unemployment, especially among the youth and vulnerable groups. Hunger was on the rise in 2010 owing mainly to rises in food prices and declines in subsidies. The combination of steep unemployment and food prices has instigated political and social unrest in some African countries. . . . The low employment content and poor social outcomes of Africa's growth are the result of lack of meaningful economic diversification and continued heavy dependence on commodity production and exports. These outcomes highlight the daunting challenges of accelerating growth and promoting structural economic transformation for Africa to achieve its social development goals.

United Nations Economic Commission for Africa,
"Economic Report on Africa 2011: Governing Development in Africa—
The Role of the State in Economic Transformation," 2011.

of working age (41 per cent) have a job, compared with 65 per cent in Brazil, 71 per cent in China and 55 per cent in India.' It goes on to calculate that 'to match the emerging markets average of 56 per cent, South Africa would need to employ 18 million people—five million more than are employed today. To keep pace with the number of people entering the labour market, this would require the economy to create about nine million jobs over the next ten years.' A tall order given contemporary trends. Moreover, the unemployment rate among all 15- to 24-year-old South Africans is 51 per cent, more than twice the national unemployment rate of 25 per cent, according to the South African Institute of Race Relations. This ratio amounts to a 'social time-bomb', as events in North Africa during 2011 illustrate. Research by the largest temporary employment services company in South Africa provides evidence that the informal sector is much bigger than hitherto assumed—8.3 million vs 2.1 million—and that the labour absorption rate is 55 per cent. The challenge still remains to generate youth employment and to move workers from the informal to the formal sector.

Although many countries in Africa have enjoyed unprecedented economic growth over the past decade, this has not translated into formal jobs.

In response, the South African government's strategy has been to leverage South Africa's comparative (i.e., the natural resource sector) advantages in conjunction with the establishment of a much tougher tax regime to generate resources to ensure redistribution to the less privileged. This has occurred both through the end of white preferences in the civil service but also the expansion of that service, along with the extension of a welfare system through pension and child-support payouts.

As in many countries, however, this leads to a bifurcated economy and society: the small numbers who are 'in' (and pay tax) and those who remain 'out' (do not pay tax) and survive and subsist in the informal economy. This not only makes building a state through a widespread tax net and base difficult, but complicates the ability to create a single society in which all citizens feel they are making a worthy contribution.

As the South African National Treasury's 2011 budget review states, 'Employment is not only about earning an income—it is the condition for a decent life.'

The Potential for Positive Change

In sub-Saharan Africa . . . despite the 2000s being the best growth decade on record, labour participation rates remain very low and informal (vulnerable) workers declined by just 0.5 per cent per annum, half as fast as East Asia and Latin America. And the continent's productivity increases were just one-quarter of those of East Asia, and less than half those of South Asia. In some cases, such as South Africa, as highlighted by the National Treasury . . . 'real wage growth . . . has out-paced growth in labour productivity.'

Without the right environment and set of opportunities, Africa's youth will likely become a destabilising force, especially in the continent's urban areas.

This is partly down to a lack of skills. While primary school enrolment rates across sub-Saharan Africa have doubled in the last generation, completion rates remain very low at under 70 per cent, compared to over 90 per cent for North Africa and East Asia. Also, the quality of education and levels of employment preparation remain poor. While Asian scores in math and science outperform developed nations, Africa lags.

Without the right environment and set of opportunities, Africa's youth will likely become a destabilising force, especially in the continent's urban areas but elsewhere too: Inevitably, many young Africans' search for a better life will take them to the cities of Europe. There is also a risk of costly populist policies. The historical record suggests that they offer much but deliver very little to alienated youth.

However, as in East Asia, where the demographic dividend was estimated to be worth as much as 40 per cent of GDP [gross domestic product] growth, if the undoubted energies of Africa's youth are correctly harnessed, and the right skills grafted, young people could be an unprecedented and tremendous force for positive change in the continent.

Unemployment in Japan Remains Low and Fairly Stable

Organisation for Economic Co-operation and Development (OECD)

In the following viewpoint, the Organisation for Economic Co-operation and Development (OECD) argues that Japan's employment market recovered quickly after the global financial crisis due to specific policies and institutions that protect against unemployment. Nonetheless, the OECD cautions that Japan's recovery has slowed and that there is risk of an increase in long-term unemployment. The OECD is an international organization whose aim is to promote policies that will improve the economic and social well-being of people around the world.

As you read, consider the following questions:

1. According to the Organisation for Economic Co-operation and Development (OECD), what was the unemployment rate in Japan in the third quarter of 2011?
2. The OECD credits what three policies for the resilience of the job market in Japan?
3. What percentage of unemployed workers in Japan had been unemployed for over a year in the last quarter of 2011, according to the OECD?

Organisation for Economic Co-operation and Development (OECD), "How Does Japan Compare?," *OECD Employment Outlook 2012*, 2012, OECD Publishing, pp. 1–2. http://www.oecd.org/employment/emp/Japan_final_EN.pdf, http://dx.doi.org/10.1787 /empl_outlook-2012-en.

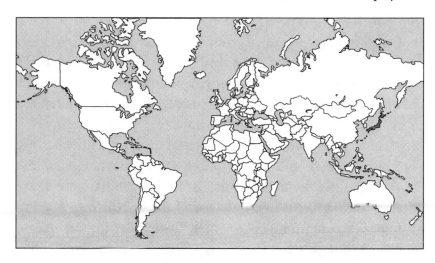

The labour market recovery in Japan began strongly but has weakened since. Since the start of the global financial crisis, the harmonised unemployment rate in Japan increased from 3.9% in the last quarter of 2007 to a cyclical peak of 5.4% in the third quarter 2009 but subsequently declined rapidly to 4.4% in the third quarter of 2011. However, the labour market recovery has slowed since and may even have come to a halt. This largely reflects the general slowdown in economic growth in Japan and many other OECD [Organisation for Economic Co-operation and Development] countries since the beginning of 2011. As of May 2012, the unemployment rate stood at 4.4%, half a percentage point higher than at the onset of the crisis. According to the OECD's projections of May 2012, the unemployment rate is expected to remain largely stable throughout the rest of 2012.

The Importance of Employment Policies

The resilience of the Japanese labour market to adverse economic shocks reflects to an important extent the role of specific policies and institutions. The Japanese labour market has performed well by OECD standards, especially given the unprecedented scale of the economic crisis and the earthquake that struck Japan. The *OECD Employment Outlook 2012* shows that also during previous economic downturns it has been consistently among the most resilient in the OECD in terms of limiting the rise in unemployment and the fall in labour income. The resilience of the Japanese labour market reflects to an important extent the importance of the long-term employment system which tends to be associated with a strong commitment by employers to preserve jobs during economic downturns; the widespread use of public short-time work schemes during the crisis (over 4% of dependent employment at its peak); and strong employment incentives for the unemployed. Although the OECD warns in its report that labour market reforms that promote the use of temporary contracts can have adverse consequences for labour market resilience, there is little evidence as of yet that the gradual liberalisation of the use of temporary contracts in the late 1990s in Japan has had a major negative impact on the resilience of its labour market.

However, long-term unemployment has risen sharply and may still be increasing. The share of workers who have been unemployed for over a year increased from 33% at the onset of the crisis to an unprecedented high of 44% in the last quarter of 2011. There has also been an increase in the number of workers who have become marginally attached to the labour force, *i.e.,* [that is,] workers who would like to work but have given up actively searching for a job. This most likely reflects the possibility that job-finding opportunities remain depressed. However, there also is a risk that some of the increase in labour market slack becomes entrenched, as a growing share of jobless workers become increasingly disconnected from the labour market and may have difficulty finding a job, even once the labour market fully recovers. Labour market policies can help contain the risk of rising unemployment by: *i)* making sure that job losers do not see their skills depreciate as a result of prolonged joblessness and will be readily employable once the labour market recovers; and *ii)* addressing any emerging structural obstacles that prevent unemployed seekers from finding jobs and employers from filling job openings.

The resilience of the Japanese labour market to adverse economic shocks reflects to an important extent the role of specific policies and institutions.

The labour share in national income has fallen substantially during the past two decades in Japan and considerably more than in most other OECD countries. Between 1990 and 2009, the labour share fell by 5.3 percentage points in Japan compared with 3.8 percentage points for the OECD area as a whole. Moreover, this trend has coincided with a substantial increase in earnings inequality. While the overall labour share declined sharply, the income share of the top 1% of earners increased. Consequently, the decline in the labour share would be even larger excluding the earnings of the top 1% of earners.

Periodical and Internet Sources Bibliography

The following articles have been selected to supplement the diverse views presented in this chapter.

Tobias Buck and Quentin Peel	"Spain's Registered Unemployed Rate Drops," *Financial Times* (UK), January 3, 2013.
John Campbell	"South Africa's Unemployment Grows," *Africa in Transition* (blog), Council on Foreign Relations, May 11, 2012. http://blogs.cfr.org.
Victor Cheung	"Jobless Rate Remains Steady at 3.4pc," *Standard* (Hong Kong), December 19, 2012.
J. Bradford DeLong	"Hopeless Unemployment," Project Syndicate, July 31, 2012. www.project-syndicate.org.
Mohamed A. El-Erian	"Sleepwalking Through America's Unemployment Crisis," Project Syndicate, May 1, 2011. www.project-syndicate.org.
Ioannis Gatsiounis	"New Africa or New Hype?," *New York Times*, May 14, 2012.
Jerusalem Post	"Poverty Poll," December 19, 2012.
Jeffrey M. Jones	"Unemployment Re-Emerges as Most Important Problem in US," Gallup.com, September 15, 2011.
Damas Kanyabwoya	"Kikwete Warns of Ticking Unemployment Bomb," Africa Review, June 1, 2012. www.africareview.com.
Glenda Kwek	"Surprise Drop in Unemployment Rate," *Sydney Morning Herald* (Australia), December 6, 2012.
Don Tapscott	"The World's Unemployed Youth: Revolution in the Air?," *Guardian* (UK), April 4, 2011.

GLOBAL VIEWPOINTS

CHAPTER 2

The Victims of Unemployment

Youth Worldwide Suffer Disproportionately from Unemployment

International Labour Organization

In the following viewpoint, the International Labour Organization (ILO) argues that the global problem of youth unemployment is not likely to improve soon. The ILO claims that high numbers of jobless youth illustrate that labor markets worldwide are weak. The ILO calls for a return to sustained economic growth as well as targeted policies to help jobless young people. The ILO is the United Nations specialized agency that seeks the promotion of social justice and internationally recognized human and labor rights.

As you read, consider the following questions:

1. According to the author, which two developed countries have youth unemployment rates over 50 percent?

2. What percentage of young European workers belong to the informal economy, according to the International Labour Organization (ILO)?

3. The ILO estimates that a job guarantee program for youth in Sweden cost less than what percentage of gross domestic product (GDP) in 2008?

Young unemployed people around the world may not see their situation improve soon. As the euro area crisis continues in its second year [2012], the impacts are spreading further, slowing down economies from East Asia to Latin America. Other regions such as sub-Saharan Africa that had expected faster improvements in their youth labour markets will now take longer to revert to levels seen prior to the global financial crisis. In developed economies, youth unemployment rates are expected to fall over the coming years, after having suffered from the largest increase among all regions at the beginning of the crisis, but principally because discouraged young people are withdrawing from the labour market and not because of stronger hiring activity among youngsters. Despite this decline and even though the young unemployed in advanced economies represent 13% of the world total, the global youth unemployment rate is expected to continue to edge higher beyond 2014.

The Problem of Youth Unemployment

In certain regions, the regional youth unemployment rate disguises large variation across countries. In particular in the Developed Economies region, youth unemployment rates range from over 50% in Spain and Greece to less than 10% in Germany and Switzerland. Even when the youth unemployment ratio is considered—the number of young unemployed in the total youth population—numbers vary from over 20% in Spain to less than 5% in Germany.

The difficulties of young people to find gainful employment reflects the overall weak state of labour markets around the world.

The deterioration in youth labour markets is also visible in other indicators. In the EU [European Union], part-time work among youth has grown faster than among adults, and

Chart 1: Global and Regional Youth Unemployment Rates (15–24 Years)

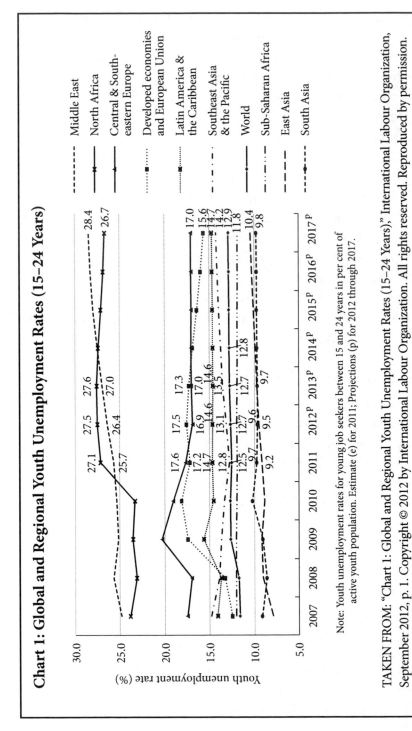

Note: Youth unemployment rates for young job seekers between 15 and 24 years in per cent of active youth population. Estimate (e) for 2011; Projections (p) for 2012 through 2017.

TAKEN FROM: "Chart 1: Global and Regional Youth Unemployment Rates (15–24 Years)," International Labour Organization, September 2012, p. 1. Copyright © 2012 by International Labour Organization. All rights reserved. Reproduced by permission.

increasingly appears to be driven by a lack of alternative employment opportunities for young people. Also, a recent analysis estimates the share of young European workers in the informal economy at about 17 per cent, compared to 7 per cent for prime age workers. On the other hand, the bleak situation for young job seekers has triggered only limited cross-border movements of young people but a lengthy and stretched-out recovery is likely to intensify the quest of young, more mobile people to seek their fortunes abroad.

The difficulties of young people to find gainful employ ment reflects the overall weak state of labour markets around the world. Global output has grown weakly over the past six months and is not expected to accelerate in the near future. As noted in the WTO's [World Trade Organization's] "World Trade Report 2012," global trade has also decelerated sharply as global demand especially in advanced economies has faltered. This has created global spillovers, leading to a slowdown of activity in emerging economies in East and South Asia and Latin America. High private and public debt in the advanced economies is leading to private households and firms deleveraging to relieve their high debt burden through increased savings rates, and austerity measures for public sectors. The combined downward pressure on both private and public consumption and investment is dragging down aggregate demand and growth. Therefore, at the current juncture there is a substantial risk that this simultaneity may trigger yet another significant downward spiral that could bring the world economy closer to another global recession by the end of 2012, further threatening a sustained labour market recovery.

The Need for Sustained Growth

Additional downward pressure on the global economy is coming from a worsening of the credit crunch that stems from unresolved sovereign debt problems in Europe. The bust of the earlier housing boom in several advanced economies together with a general need for deleveraging in the private sector left banks with unsustainable levels of non-performing loans, forcing some governments to bail out their distressed banks. This transferred private debt into public. The ensuing increase in interest payments and a general distrust in the capacity of the public sector to successfully manage this enhanced debt burden has compelled these governments into several rounds of austerity to reduce their borrowing costs. As a result, and despite highly accommodative monetary policy, the combination of skyrocketing risk premiums for long-term loans and depressed aggregate demand due to fiscal austerity measures have prevented both the private and the public sectors in these countries from recovering and creating new jobs.

Looking ahead, a pre-condition for improvement in youth unemployment is a return to a sustained growth path and a general strengthening of the labour market.

Moreover, structural imbalances that were built up prior to the crisis have worsened, further slowing the recovery. Indeed, even in countries with first signs of a jobs recovery and where firms started to open new vacancies, many unemployed have had difficulties in landing a job. This is partly linked to the shift in sectoral demand that countries with a bust housing sector face: As employment in sectors such as construction declines new sectors with different skill requirements may not be able to absorb the unemployed from these shrinking sectors. In some countries with high youth unemployment rates, this is a particularly harsh problem leading to discouragement and rising NEET rates ("neither in employment, education nor training") among young people.

Looking ahead, a pre-condition for improvement in youth unemployment is a return to a sustained growth path and a general strengthening of the labour market. Without additional jobs being created, young people cannot expect to find employment. However, given the sheer size of the problem, even a quick acceleration in growth may not provide sufficient job opportunities in a short period of time. To address this, the ILO [International Labour Organization] is calling for targeted measures to improve the labour market situation, especially for youth. For example, providing employment or training guarantees for (targeted groups of) young people—such as those that currently exist in several countries—could help get young job seekers off the street and into useful activities and act as a safeguard against further economic and social stress. Estimates show that such programmes can come at very limited costs, less than half a per cent of GDP [gross domestic product] among European countries, depending on administrative costs and actual take-up

This is consistent with costs observed in existing youth employment guarantee programmes, such as those enacted in Austria, Denmark, Finland, Norway and Sweden. In Sweden, a job guarantee programme for youth enacted in the 1980s and reformed in 2007 combined active labour market policies (such as intensive job matching efforts and further skills development) with payroll tax cuts for employers hiring young people. This programme was estimated to cost less than 0.1% of GDP in 2008. Broader employment guarantee programmes targeting persons of all ages living in poor households have also been enacted in some countries, most notably India. The cost of India's national rural employment guarantee programme has been estimated at around 1% of GDP. In times of constrained public finances, this may seem like a large additional burden but it will be less than the additional costs that come from young unemployed people permanently losing touch with the labour market.

Youth Unemployment Worldwide Is Not as Bad as Is Often Stated

Steven Hill

In the following viewpoint, Steven Hill argues that the way the official unemployment rate is measured results in misleading numbers. Hill claims that a more meaningful indicator of measuring and assessing economic health is the unemployment ratio, which measures the unemployed in relation to the total population rather than to those considered part of the labor force. Hill claims that unemployment ratios in Europe are much less alarming than unemployment rates. Hill is a political writer, columnist, and policy analyst. He is the author of Europe's Promise: Why the European Way Is the Best Hope in an Insecure Age.

As you read, consider the following questions:

1. According to Hill, flawed methodology supports youth unemployment estimates of more than 50 percent in what two countries?

2. What is the euro zone–wide unemployment rate compared with its unemployment ratio, according to Hill?

3. The author claims that in 2006 France's high youth unemployment rate but low youth unemployment ratio is explained by what fact?

Economists worldwide need better ways to measure economic activity. Relying on GDP [gross domestic product] growth rates to assess economic health, almost all of them missed the warning signs of the 2008 financial crisis, including an $8 trillion real-estate bubble in the United States, as well as property bubbles in Spain, Ireland, and the United Kingdom. Together with households, financial institutions, investors, and governments, economists were swept up in the financial euphoria that led to excessive risk taking and severe over-leveraging of banks and households. Even the euro zone's macroeconomic imbalances largely went unnoticed.

How Unemployment Is Measured

Unemployment estimates also are surprisingly misleading—a serious problem, considering that, together with GDP indicators, unemployment drives so much economic policy debate. Outrageously high youth unemployment—supposedly near 50% in Spain and Greece, and more than 20% in the euro zone as a whole—makes headlines daily. But these numbers result from flawed methodology, making the situation appear far worse than it is.

The problem stems from how unemployment is measured: The adult unemployment rate is calculated by dividing the number of unemployed individuals by all individuals in the labor force. So if the labor force comprises 200 workers and 20 are unemployed, the unemployment rate is 10%.

But the millions of young people who attend university or vocational training programs are not considered part of the labor force, because they are neither working nor looking for a job. In calculating youth unemployment, therefore, the same number of unemployed individuals is divided by a much smaller number, to reflect the smaller labor force, which makes the unemployment rate look a lot higher.

In the example above, let us say that 150 of the 200 workers become full-time university students. Only 50 individuals

---

The Official Statistics on Unemployment

The official statistics can ... be misleading. Far fewer than half of Spanish under-25s are languishing without jobs. The unemployment rate seeks only to measure the proportion out of work relative to those active in the labour market. Those in college do not count, and a large proportion counted in the official figures are in full-time education.

Chris Giles, *"Soaring Youth Unemployment Stokes Fears,"* Financial Times *(UK), July 2, 2012.*

---

remain in the labor force. Although the number of unemployed people remains at 20, the unemployment rate quadruples, to 40%. So the perverse result of this way of counting the unemployed is that the more young people who pursue additional education or training, the higher the youth unemployment rate rises.

The problem stems from how unemployment is measured.

While standard measures exaggerate youth unemployment, they likely understate adult unemployment, because those who have given up their job search are not counted among the unemployed. As the Great Recession drives up the number of such "discouraged workers," adult unemployment rates appear to fall—presenting a distorted picture of reality.

A Better Methodology

Fortunately, there is a better methodology: The youth unemployment *ratio*—the number of unemployed youth relative to the total population aged 16–24—is a far more meaningful indicator than the youth unemployment rate. Eurostat, the European Union's statistical agency, calculates youth unemployment using both methodologies, but only the flawed indicator is widely reported, despite major discrepancies. For example, Spain's 48.9% youth unemployment rate implies significantly worse conditions for young people than its 19% youth unemployment ratio. Likewise, Greece's rate is 49.3%, but its ratio is only 13%. And the euro zone–wide rate of 20.8% far exceeds the 8.7% ratio.

To be sure, a youth unemployment ratio of 13% or 19% is not grounds for complacency. But, while the eurozone's youth unemployment rate has increased since 2009, its ratio has remained the same (though both significantly exceed pre-2008 levels).

Failing to account for the millions of young people either attending university or in vocational training programs undermines the unemployment rate's credibility.

During the 2006 French student protests, France's 22% youth unemployment rate appeared to compare unfavorably to rates of 11%, 12%, and 13% in the United Kingdom, the US, and Germany, respectively. But the *Financial Times* showed that only 7.8% of French under-25s were unemployed—about the same ratio as in the other three countries. France simply had a higher percentage of young people who were full-time students.

The Credibility of the Unemployment Rate

Failing to account for the millions of young people either attending university or in vocational training programs undermines the unemployment rate's credibility. And, while some young people use higher education to escape a rocky job market, their choice to build new skills should not negatively impact perceptions of their country's economic health.

Policy makers do, of course, need to address the problem of youth unemployment; but they must also acknowledge that the problem is not as serious as the headlines indicate. Unfortunately, these distorted results have become conventional wisdom—even for respected economists like the Nobel laureate Paul Krugman, who recently invoked the flawed "50% youth unemployment" figure.

Thus, four years after the crisis erupted, methods for measuring and assessing economic health remain alarmingly inadequate. As any pilot knows, flying without radar or accurate weather forecasts is likely to end in a crash.

In the United States, Men Suffer from High Rates of Unemployment

Don Peck

In the following viewpoint, Don Peck argues that it will take years to resolve the legacy of joblessness left behind by the Great Recession. Peck claims that certain populations, such as lower income men, have been particularly hard hit. Peck contends that the impact of chronic unemployment of these men on marriage, children, and society could be a long-term catastrophe if not remedied soon. Peck is a features editor for the Atlantic *and the author of* Pinched: How the Great Recession Has Narrowed Our Futures and What We Can Do About It.

As you read, consider the following questions:

1. According to the author, a recent survey showed what percentage of American families experiencing job loss, reduction in work hours, or a pay cut in the previous year?

2. In November 2009, what percentage of men aged twenty-five to fifty-four were without employment, according to Peck?

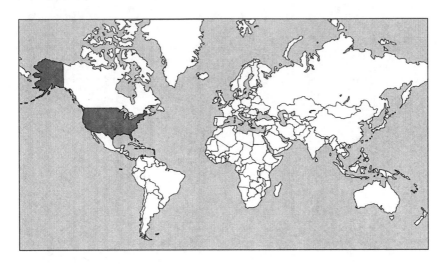

3. According to the author, approximately what fraction of new mothers without a college degree are unmarried?

How should we characterize the economic period we have now entered? After nearly two brutal years [2008–2010], the Great Recession appears to be over, at least technically. Yet a return to normalcy seems far off. By some measures, each recession since the 1980s has retreated more slowly than the one before it. In one sense, we never fully recovered from the last one, in 2001: The share of the civilian population with a job never returned to its previous peak before this downturn began, and incomes were stagnant throughout the decade. Still, the weakness that lingered through much of the 2000s shouldn't be confused with the trauma of the past two years, a trauma that will remain heavy for quite some time.

The unemployment rate hit 10 percent in October [2009], and there are good reasons to believe that by 2011, 2012, even 2014, it will have declined only a little. Late last year, the average duration of unemployment surpassed six months, the first time that has happened since 1948, when the Bureau of Labor Statistics began tracking that number. As of this writing [March 2010], for every open job in the U.S., six people are actively looking for work.

The Dangers of Chronic Unemployment

All of these figures understate the magnitude of the jobs crisis. The broadest measure of unemployment and underemployment (which includes people who want to work but have stopped actively searching for a job, along with those who want full-time jobs but can find only part-time work) reached 17.4 percent in October, which appears to be the highest figure since the 1930s. And for large swaths of society—young adults, men, minorities—that figure was much higher (among teenagers, for instance, even the narrowest measure of unemployment stood at roughly 27 percent). One recent survey showed that 44 percent of families had experienced a job loss, a reduction in hours, or a pay cut in the past year.

There is unemployment, a brief and relatively routine transitional state that results from the rise and fall of companies in any economy, and there is *unemployment*—chronic, all-consuming. The former is a necessary lubricant in any engine of economic growth. The latter is a pestilence that slowly eats away at people, families, and, if it spreads widely enough, the fabric of society. Indeed, history suggests that it is perhaps society's most noxious ill.

The worst effects of pervasive joblessness—on family, politics, society—take time to incubate, and they show themselves only slowly. But ultimately, they leave deep marks that endure long after boom times have returned. Some of these marks are just now becoming visible, and even if the economy magically and fully recovers tomorrow, new ones will continue to appear. The longer our economic slump lasts, the deeper they'll be.

If it persists much longer, this era of high joblessness will likely change the life course and character of a generation of young adults—and quite possibly those of the children behind them as well. It will leave an indelible imprint on many blue-collar white men—and on white culture. It could change the nature of modern marriage, and also cripple marriage as an institution in many communities. It may already be plunging many inner cities into a kind of despair and dysfunction not seen for decades. Ultimately, it is likely to warp our politics, our culture, and the character of our society for years.

The worst effects of pervasive joblessness—on family, politics, society—take time to incubate, and they show themselves only slowly.

The Predictions of Economic Recovery

Since last spring, when fears of economic apocalypse began to ebb, we've been treated to an alphabet soup of predictions about the recovery. Various economists have suggested that it might look like a *V* (a strong and rapid rebound), a *U* (slower), a *W* (reflecting the possibility of a double-dip recession), or, most alarming, an *L* (no recovery in demand or jobs for years: a lost decade). This summer, with all the good letters already taken, the former labor secretary Robert Reich wrote on his blog that the recovery might actually be shaped like an *X* (the imagery is elusive, but Reich's argument was that there can be no recovery until we find an entirely new model of economic growth).

No one knows what shape the recovery will take. The economy grew at an annual rate of 2.2 percent in the third quarter of last year, the first increase since the second quarter of 2008. If economic growth continues to pick up, substantial job growth will eventually follow. But there are many reasons to doubt the durability of the economic turnaround, and the speed with which jobs will return.

Historically, financial crises have spawned long periods of economic malaise, and this crisis, so far, has been true to form. Despite the bailouts, many banks' balance sheets remain weak; more than 140 banks failed in 2009. As a result, banks have kept lending standards tight, frustrating the efforts of small businesses—which have accounted for almost half of all job losses—to invest or rehire. Exports seem unlikely to provide much of a boost; although China, India, Brazil, and some other emerging markets are growing quickly again. Europe and Japan—both major markets for U.S. exports—remain weak. And in any case, exports make up only about 13 percent of total U.S. production; even if they were to grow quickly, the impact would be muted.

Most recessions end when people start spending again, but for the foreseeable future, U.S. consumer demand is unlikely to propel strong economic growth. As of November, one in seven mortgages was delinquent, up from one in 10 a year earlier. As many as one in four houses may now be underwater [meaning the home loan is higher than the home's market value], and the ratio of household debt to GDP [gross domestic product], about 65 percent in the mid-1990s, is roughly 100 percent today. It is not merely animal spirits that are keeping people from spending freely (though those spirits are dour). Heavy debt and large losses of wealth have forced spending onto a lower path.

The Need for Economic Growth

So what is the engine that will pull the U.S. back onto a strong growth path? That turns out to be a hard question. The *New York Times* columnist Paul Krugman, who fears a lost decade, said in a lecture at the London School of Economics [and Political Science] last summer that he has "no idea" how the economy could quickly return to strong, sustainable growth. Mark Zandi, the chief economist at Moody's Economy.com, told the Associated Press last fall, "I think the unemployment rate will be permanently higher, or at least higher for the foreseeable future. The collective psyche has changed as a result of what we've been through. And we're going to be different as a result."

One big reason that the economy stabilized last summer and fall is the stimulus; the Congressional Budget Office estimates that without the stimulus, growth would have been anywhere from 1.2 to 3.2 percentage points lower in the third quarter of 2009. The stimulus will continue to trickle into the economy for the next couple of years, but as a concentrated force, it's largely spent. Christina Romer, the chair of President [Barack] Obama's Council of Economic Advisers, said last fall, "By mid-2010, fiscal stimulus will likely be contributing little to further growth," adding that she didn't expect unemployment to fall significantly until 2011. That prediction has since been echoed, more or less, by the Federal Reserve and Goldman Sachs.

The economy now sits in a hole more than 10 million jobs deep—that's the number required to get back to 5 percent unemployment, the rate we had before the recession started, and one that's been more or less typical for a generation. And because the population is growing and new people are continually coming onto the job market, we need to produce roughly 1.5 million new jobs a year—about 125,000 a month—just to keep from sinking deeper.

The economy now sits in a hole more than 10 million jobs deep—that's the number required to get back to 5 percent unemployment, the rate we had before the recession started.

Even if the economy were to immediately begin producing 600,000 jobs a month—more than double the pace of the mid-to-late 1990s, when job growth was strong—it would take roughly two years to dig ourselves out of the hole we're in. The economy could add jobs that fast, or even faster—job growth is theoretically limited only by labor supply, and a lot more labor is sitting idle today than usual. But the U.S. hasn't seen that pace of sustained employment growth in more than

30 years. And given the particulars of this recession, matching idle workers with new jobs—even once economic growth picks up—seems likely to be a particularly slow and challenging process. . . .

Unemployment and Gender

The weight of this recession has fallen most heavily upon men, who've suffered roughly three-quarters of the 8 million job losses since the beginning of 2008. Male-dominated industries (construction, finance, manufacturing) have been particularly hard hit, while sectors that disproportionately employ women (education, health care) have held up relatively well. In November, 19.4 percent of all men in their prime working years, 25 to 54, did not have jobs, the highest figure since the Bureau of Labor Statistics began tracking the statistic in 1948. At the time of this writing, it looks possible that within the next few months, for the first time in U.S. history, women will hold a majority of the country's jobs.

In this respect, the recession has merely intensified a long-standing trend. Broadly speaking, the service sector, which employs relatively more women, is growing, while manufacturing, which employs relatively more men, is shrinking. The net result is that men have been contributing a smaller and smaller share of family income.

"Traditional" marriages, in which men engage in paid work and women in homemaking, have long been in eclipse. Particularly in blue-collar families, where many husbands and wives work staggered shifts, men routinely handle a lot of the child care today. Still, the ease with which gender bends in modern marriages should not be overestimated. When men stop doing paid work—and even when they work less than their wives—marital conflict usually follows.

Unemployed Men and Marital Conflict

Last March, the National Domestic Violence Hotline received almost half as many calls as it had one year earlier; as was the

The Decline in Male Employment

Forty years ago, virtually all men with at least a high school degree held jobs. Most high school dropouts worked, too. Most men, regardless of education, could make a decent living, and holding a job was the unquestioned norm. Any man who didn't work for years at a stretch was known as a bum.

Since then, men have been steadily withdrawing from the workforce—but, again, not uniformly. Ninety percent of college-educated men are still working. But a fifth of men with only a high school degree weren't working in 2008, before the recession struck; today, a fourth of them don't hold a job. Among men who didn't finish high school, a third aren't working. As a result of these trends, America today is pockmarked with neighborhoods where nonwork is the male norm.

Jonathan Rauch,
"The No Good, Very Bad Outlook for the Working-Class
American Man," National Journal, *December 5, 2012.*

case in the Depression, unemployed men are vastly more likely to beat their wives or children. More common than violence, though, is a sort of passive-aggressiveness. In *Identity Economics*, the economists George [A.] Akerlof and Rachel [E.] Kranton find that among married couples, men who aren't working at all, despite their free time, do only 37 percent of the housework, on average. And some men, apparently in an effort to guard their masculinity, actually do less housework after becoming unemployed.

Many working women struggle with the idea of partners who aren't breadwinners. "We've got this image of Archie Bunker sitting at home, grumbling and acting out," says Kathryn Edin, a professor of public policy at Harvard, and an expert on family life. "And that does happen. But you also have women in whole communities thinking, 'This guy's nothing.'" Edin's research in low-income communities shows, for instance, that most working women whose partner stayed home to watch the kids—while very happy with the quality of child care their children's father provided—were dissatisfied with their relationship overall. "These relationships were often filled with conflict," Edin told me. Even today, she says, men's identities are far more defined by their work than women's, and both men and women become extremely uncomfortable when men's work goes away.

The national divorce rate fell slightly in 2008, and that's not unusual in a recession: Divorce is expensive, and many couples delay it in hard times. But joblessness corrodes marriages and makes divorce much more likely down the road. According to W. Bradford Wilcox, the director of the National Marriage Project at the University of Virginia, the gender imbalance of the job losses in this recession is particularly noteworthy, and—when combined with the depth and duration of the jobs crisis—poses "a profound challenge to marriage," especially in lower-income communities. It may sound harsh, but in general, he says, "if men can't make a contribution financially, they don't have much to offer." Two-thirds of all divorces are legally initiated by women. Wilcox believes that over the next few years, we may see a long wave of divorces, washing no small number of discarded and dispirited men back into single adulthood.

Among couples without college degrees, says Edin, marriage has become an "increasingly fragile" institution. In many low-income communities, she fears it is being supplanted as a social norm by single motherhood and revolving-door relationships. As a rule, fewer people marry during a recession, and this one has been no exception. But "the timing of this recession coincides with a pretty significant cultural change," Edin says: a fast-rising material threshold for marrying, but not for having children, in less affluent communities.

Joblessness corrodes marriages and makes divorce much more likely down the road.

Edin explains that poor and working-class couples, after seeing the ravages of divorce on their parents or within their communities, have become more hesitant to marry; they believe deeply in marriage's sanctity, and try to guard against the possibility that theirs will end in divorce. Studies have shown that even small changes in income have significant effects on marriage rates among the poor and the lower middle class. "It's simply not respectable to get married if you don't have a job—some way of illustrating to your neighbors that you have at least some grasp on some piece of the American pie," Edin says. Increasingly, people in these communities see marriage not as a way to build savings and stability, but as "a symbol that you've arrived."

The Impact on Children

Childbearing is the opposite story. The stigma against out-of-wedlock children has by now largely dissolved in working-class communities—more than half of all new mothers without a college degree are unmarried. For both men and women in these communities, children are commonly seen as a highly desirable, relatively low-cost way to achieve meaning and bolster identity—especially when other opportunities are closed off. Christina Gibson-Davis, a public policy professor at Duke University, recently found that among adults with no college degree, changes in income have no bearing at all on rates of childbirth.

"We already have low marriage rates in low-income communities," Edin told me, "including white communities. And where it's really hitting now is in working-class urban and rural communities, where you're just seeing astonishing growth in the rates of nonmarital childbearing. And that would all be fine and good, except these parents don't stay together. This may be one of the most devastating impacts of the recession."

Many children are already suffering in this recession, for a variety of reasons. Among poor families, nutrition can be inadequate in hard times, hampering children's mental and physical development. And regardless of social class, the stresses and distractions that afflict unemployed parents also afflict their kids, who are more likely to repeat a grade in school, and who on average earn less as adults. Children with unemployed fathers seem particularly vulnerable to psychological problems.

The Demise of Entire Communities

But a large body of research shows that one of the worst things for children, in the long run, is an unstable family. By the time the average out-of-wedlock child has reached the age of 5, his or her mother will have had two or three significant relationships with men other than the father, and the child will typically have at least one half sibling. This kind of churning is terrible for children—heightening the risks of mental health problems, troubles at school, teenage delinquency, and so on—and we're likely to see more and more of it, the longer this malaise stretches on.

Communities with large numbers of unmarried, jobless men take on an unsavory character over time.

"We could be headed in a direction where, among elites, marriage and family are conventional, but for substantial portions of society, life is more matriarchal," says Wilcox. The marginalization of working-class men in family life has far-reaching consequences. "Marriage plays an important role in civilizing men. They work harder, longer, more strategically. They spend less time in bars and more time in church, less with friends and more with kin. And they're happier and healthier."

Communities with large numbers of unmarried, jobless men take on an unsavory character over time. Edin's research team spent part of last summer in Northeast and South Philadelphia, conducting in-depth interviews with residents. She says she was struck by what she saw: "These white working-class communities—once strong, vibrant, proud communities, often organized around big industries—they're just in terrible straits. The social fabric of these places is just shredding. There's little engagement in religious life, and the old civic organizations that people used to belong to are fading. Drugs have ravaged these communities, along with divorce, alcoholism, violence. I hang around these neighborhoods in South Philadelphia, and I think, 'This is beginning to look like the black inner-city neighborhoods we've been studying for the past 20 years.' When young men can't transition into formal-sector jobs, they sell drugs and drink and do drugs. And it wreaks havoc on family life. They think, 'Hey, if I'm 23 and I don't have a baby, there's something wrong with me.' They're following the pattern of their fathers in terms of the timing of childbearing, but they don't have the jobs to support it. So their families are falling apart—and often spectacularly.". . .

A National Catastrophe

A slowly sinking generation; a remorseless assault on the identity of many men; the dissolution of families and the collapse of neighborhoods; a thinning veneer of national amity—the social legacies of the Great Recession are still being written, but their breadth and depth are immense. As problems, they are enormously complex, and their solutions will be equally so.

Of necessity, those solutions must include measures to bolster the economy in the short term, and to clear the way for faster long-term growth; to support the jobless today, and to ensure that we are creating the kinds of jobs (and the kinds of skills within the population) that can allow for a more broadly shared prosperity in the future. A few of the solutions—like more aggressive support for the unemployed, and employer tax credits or other subsidies to get people back to work faster—are straightforward and obvious, or at least they should be. Many are not.

We are living through a slow-motion social catastrophe, one that could stain our culture and weaken our nation for many, many years to come.

At the very least, though, we should make the return to a more normal jobs environment an unflagging national priority. The stock market has rallied, the financial system has stabilized, and job losses have slowed; by the time you read this, the unemployment rate might be down a little. Yet the difference between "turning the corner" and a return to any sort of normalcy is vast.

We are in a very deep hole, and we've been in it for a relatively long time already. Concerns over deficits are understandable, but in these times, our bias should be toward doing too much rather than doing too little. That implies some small risk to the government's ability to continue borrowing in the future; and it implies somewhat higher taxes in the future too. But that seems a trade worth making. We are living through a slow-motion social catastrophe, one that could stain our culture and weaken our nation for many, many years to come. We have a civic—and indeed a moral—responsibility to do everything in our power to stop it now, before it gets even worse.

In Mexico, Unemployment Is Highest for Young Women

Guadalupe Cruz Jaime

In the following viewpoint, Guadalupe Cruz Jaime argues that work prospects in Mexico are bleak, especially for young women, whether they are educated or not. Jaime claims that unemployment is expected to climb, with most of the job losses hitting industries dominated by women. Jaime contends that the jobs crisis causes women to migrate to the United States illegally rather than remain in Mexico where even those women with jobs have a hard time meeting basic needs. Jaime is a journalist for the Inter Press Service (IPS) news agency.

As you read, consider the following questions:

1. Women make up what portion of the textile industry, according to the author?
2. The author cites a statistic showing what fraction of Mexican immigrants to the United States are women?
3. Compensation in wages, salaries, and benefits for the retail sales sector dropped by what fraction from 2005 to 2011, according to the author?

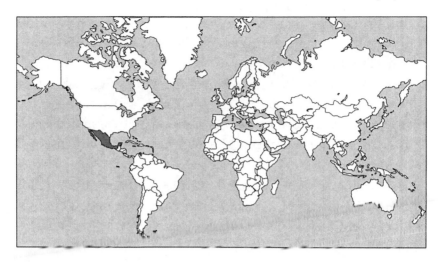

The year 2012 started off with little promise for workers in Mexico, with analysts projecting job losses and wages below subsistence levels. Work prospects arc even bleaker for young women, whose chances of finding a job are no better with a high school diploma or university degree.

Unemployment in Mexico

Carmen Ponce, an economist specialising in gender issues, says 2012 will be a "very challenging" year for Mexico in terms of job creation, as Chinese goods begin flooding the country as a result of the implementation of a trade agreement that opens the door to imports from China.

Ponce forecasts that around 100,000 jobs will be lost this year. The sectors most "severely" affected will be the textile, shoe and toy industries, where women dominate the workforce. In the textile industry alone, they account for 70% of all workers.

Young women are the hardest hit by jobs cuts, with figures climbing from 7% in the second quarter of 2007 to 10% in the same period of 2011 among women aged 14 to 19. Unemployment in this age group is also "indicating that family incomes are so low that [young women] are having to venture into the job market to bring in another salary, instead of staying in school", Ponce said.

Among 20- to 29-year-old women with high school or university studies, the increase is similarly "alarming", steadily rising from almost 8% in 2007 to more than 10% in 2011. For Ponce, these figures reflect "the feminisation of unemployment".

According to the National [Institute of] Statistics and Geography (Inegi), as of November 2011 there were 2.8 million people unemployed in Mexico, and seven out of 10 had secondary or higher education.

Young women are the hardest hit by jobs cuts.

The Migration of Mexican Women

The lack of opportunities has driven many to migrate to the United States. Ponce notes that more and more young people with more than nine years of schooling are migrating to the US, risking their lives as they cross the border illegally. Of the 767 migrants reported dead in 2011, 62% were young women.

A report by a legal committee of the opposition Institutional Revolutionary Party (PRI) in congress found that most of these women had completed secondary or higher studies.

According to Inegi, three out of 10 Mexicans who migrate to the US are women.

The PRI report, prepared with the Office for Migration Matters of the NGO [nongovernmental organisation] National Confederation of Grassroots Organizations, further reveals that 75% of the migrants who died in 2011 had completed primary school.

Sixty per cent of the 767 deaths were violent, with victims either mugged, raped, abandoned in the desert by migrant smugglers, or targeted by organised crime.

According to the report, unemployment is highest among the most educated women, who, faced with no work opportunities, have to choose between migrating to the US, joining the ranks of the underemployed, or swelling the informal job market.

A Bleak Outlook

Ponce notes that things will only get worse as a result of the economic recession in the US and Europe, which is compounded by Mexico's low rate of job creation. With a population of 112 million, Mexico requires around 1.5 to 2m new jobs each year.

The economic modelling and forecasting centre of the National Autonomous University of Mexico (Unam) projects that unemployment will be as high as 6.1% this year, up from 5.7% in 2011, and, as a result, the quality of job opportunities will "plunge", Ponce said.

Mexican women who do find employment will have to settle for poor working conditions and wages too low to cover even the basic food basket. In the retail sales sector, for example, which employs 4.4 million of the country's 18 million women workers, real compensation (wages, salaries and benefits) has plummeted, dropping by almost 25% between 2005 and 2011.

The 18 cents raise approved by the National Minimum Wage [Commission] is thus inadequate, as the rise in prices of basic goods "grossly" exceeds it, labour experts say. From 2006 to 2011 the cost of the basic food basket more than doubled, from $5.80 to $12.60 a day, while the minimum wage increased by a mere 83 cents, according to data from the multi-disciplinary analysis centre of Unam's School of Economics.

The situation is especially critical for the 27% of Mexican homes that are headed by women, as they earn only around 70% of what men earn for the same task and with the same level of education, according to data from the Economic Commission for Latin America and the Caribbean.

Chinese Survey Finds Higher Jobless Rate

Tom Orlik

In the following viewpoint, Tom Orlik argues that a new survey on unemployment in China shows that the method of counting the unemployed fails to account for a large number of job losses among migrant workers. Orlik claims that compared with Europe and the United States, China has relatively low unemployment. Nonetheless, he claims that the failure to count unemployed migrant workers and the long-term unemployed masks real job losses. Orlik is a China correspondent for the Wall Street Journal *in Beijing, where he writes the Heard on the Street column.*

As you read, consider the following questions:

1. According to Orlik, what percentage of migrant workers were unemployed in June 2012?

2. How many migrant worker jobs were lost in China in 2012, according to the author?

3. How many fewer state sector jobs existed in China in 2002 compared to 1992, according to Orlik?

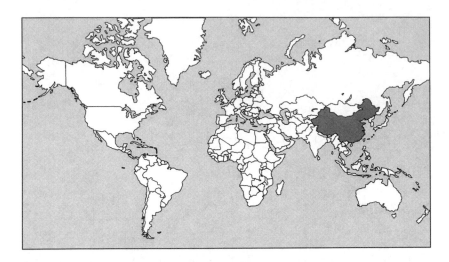

Beijing—A new survey shows that the real unemployment rate in China is double the official level, and layoffs rose sharply among migrant workers in the past year [2012], underlining a challenge for China's new leaders to maintain growth.

The survey of 8,000 households shows the urban unemployment rate hit 8.05% in June, up slightly from 8% in August 2011 and nearly twice as high as the official 4.1% rate. The survey was run by Gan Li, an economics professor at Southwestern University of Finance and Economics in Chengdu.

The unemployment rate for China's army of 160 million migrant workers has risen sharply to 6% in June 2012, up from 3.4% in August 2011 according to the survey, suggesting 10 million unemployed as a result of the sharp slowdown in exports and real estate construction.

The survey represents the most ambitious attempt yet to map China's labor markets, household income and asset ownership—areas where the official data are widely regarded as inaccurate or deficient.

Employment is a hot-button issue for China's ruling Communist Party, with the risk that high levels of joblessness could trigger destabilizing unrest. At the end of 2008, severe job losses for migrant workers helped prompt the government to unleash a massive stimulus package.

The unemployment rate for China's army of 160 million migrant workers has risen sharply.

In 2012, as migrant-worker unemployment has increased, the government has taken steps to buoy growth, speeding approval of projects from city subways to steel mills, and cutting interest rates twice over the summer.

Similarly, high unemployment for urban residents helps explain the government's reluctance to push ahead with needed structural reforms. Minxin Pei, a China expert at Claremont McKenna College, says that revamping the state-owned sector to operate in a more commercial fashion could cost as many as four million jobs initially.

China's official unemployment rate is based on urban residents registering for unemployment benefits. That measure leaves out key sections of the workforce—notably migrant workers, who go uncounted because they can't register for such benefits in the cities where they go to work. For the last 15 years it has stayed in a tight range between 3.1% and 4.3%, failing to capture wrenching changes in China's labor markets.

Mr. Gan's survey attempts to overcome the problems of the official data by dispatching student researchers into households up and down the country.

Despite a significantly higher rate of unemployment than reported by the government, China's labor market still appears to have weathered 2012's growth slowdown relatively well. A loss of around 4.5 million jobs for China's migrant workers in the past year has taken their unemployment level to 10 million, still well below the 23 million out of work in 2009.

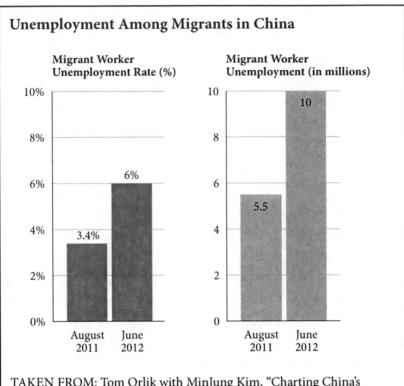

Unemployment Among Migrants in China

Migrant Worker Unemployment Rate (%)

Migrant Worker Unemployment (in millions)

TAKEN FROM: Tom Orlik with MinJung Kim, "Charting China's Family Value," *Wall Street Journal*, December 10, 2012. blogs.wsj.com.

With no access to urban social benefits, migrant workers typically respond to job losses by either returning to the farm or accepting lower pay. A separate survey by Xin Meng of Australian National University shows migrant-worker wage growth slowed to 1.7% year-on-year in 2012, from 23% in 2011.

China's economy has also escaped the rapid increase in unemployment that has plagued the U.S. and European economies since the financial crisis. Though it is likely that some of the workers classified as unemployed by Mr. Gan's survey would be counted among those no longer looking for work in the U.S. The U.S. jobless rate was 7.7% in November, but a broader measure that includes discouraged workers and those involuntarily stuck in part-time jobs was at 14.4%.

For younger workers, with higher skills, China's unemployment rate remains low—4.1% for those with a vocational degree according to the survey.

The number of job opportunities advertised on Zhaopin.com, China's biggest recruitment website, has risen 10%–15% this year, a slowdown from 30% growth in 2011 says chief executive Evan Guo, "but job opportunities are still increasing."

Albert Park, a China labor market expert at Hong Kong University of Science and Technology, says a 2010 survey conducted with the Chinese Academy of Social Sciences of 6,500 households in five large cities found an unemployment rate of 2.4% for urban residents and 0.7% for migrant workers. That survey employed the international standard definition for unemployment—excluding discouraged workers.

Some who lost their jobs in the state sector, notably those from China's northeast rust belt, joined the rural migrants working for pennies on the production lines.

The survey also reflects China's hidden army of long-term unemployed: workers laid off in the late 1990s when the government closed thousands of unprofitable state enterprises, who haven't managed to find work since. For men aged 51–60 with urban residence, the unemployment rate is 27.5%. Since many of these laid-off former state sector workers continue to receive some form of compensation from their former employers, they aren't counted in the official unemployment data.

From a peak of 145.1 million in 1992, the number of jobs in China's state sector fell to 82.8 million in 2002. At the same time, a wave of migrant workers were setting out from farms in inland provinces like Henan and Sichuan, looking for jobs in the private sector factories that were driving China's export boom.

Some who lost their jobs in the state sector, notably those from China's northeast rust belt, joined the rural migrants working for pennies on the production lines. But others were unwilling to work for the same low wages as rural migrants, or saw sweatshop work as beneath their dignity. They faced up to a life on benefits, and temporary work as security guards, taxi drivers, and cleaners.

Yang Ronghua, a 49-year-old woman from Baoding in Hebei province, worked in a collectively owned auto-parts factory through the 1980s and '90s. "Ten years ago, our factory stopped operating. Since then I have no work, just temporary jobs," she said.

Ms. Yang and her husband survive on her husband's meager 1,200 yuan ($193) a month salary, and a small lump-sum compensation payment she received from the factory. "It's hard for a woman over 40, with no skills, to find a job," said Ms. Yang.

However, as this cohort hit retirement age and start to leave the labor force, the level of unemployment will fall.

—Kersten Zhang contributed to this article.

In Australia, the Unemployed Do Not Receive Enough Benefits

Suzy Freeman-Greene

In the following viewpoint, Suzy Freeman-Greene argues that the current amount of unemployment benefits in Australia, called the Newstart Allowance, is too low to allow people to meet basic needs and find work. Freeman-Greene contends that begging and stealing by many unemployed Australians may be the result of overly stingy benefits. She questions fairness of a society that offers generous government assistance to the wealthy, but fails to adequately provide for the poorest unemployed. Freeman-Greene is a senior writer at the Age, *a daily newspaper in Melbourne, Australia.*

As you read, consider the following questions:

1. According to Freeman-Greene, what is the weekly benefit amount for an unemployed single individual in Australia?

2. What percentage of unemployment benefits recipients in Australia are renters, according to the author?

3. The richest fifth of Australian households receive what portion of government assistance, according to Freeman-Greene?

Suzy Freeman-Greene, "The Poor Get Poorer While the Rest Get the Handouts," *The Age* (Australia), December 15, 2012. Reproduced by permission.

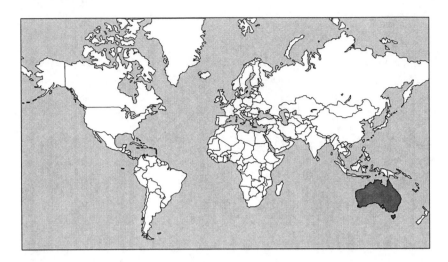

When will [Australian prime minister] Julia Gillard's government find the courage to raise the dole [unemployment benefits]? Her party's website tells us it is working for a "fairer Australia". But while middle-class welfare endures, our poorest citizens are living far below the poverty line.

Unemployment Benefits in Australia

We've been hearing the figures for so long that they've become a kind of mantra. Single adults on the Newstart Allowance [Australia's government unemployment benefits] live on about $35 [Australian dollars, equal to approximately 36 US dollars] a day. That's $246 a week. Pensioners now get $386 a week. The poverty line for a single person is $358 a week.

While middle-class welfare endures, our poorest citizens are living far below the poverty line.

The Business Council of Australia and economist Ken Henry—hardly bleeding hearts—have called for the dole to be raised, along with unions and welfare groups. St Vincent de Paul's Dr John Falzon has said it's a matter of deep shame that unemployment benefits are kept low deliberately "as a means of humiliating the very people they were originally designed to assist".

A Senate committee investigating the matter received moving submissions on the dole's inadequacy but couldn't bring itself to recommend an increase. It's chairman, Liberal senator Chris Back, later told the *Age* journalist Peter Martin there was a "compelling" case for increasing Newstart. But it seems that since his party might be in government soon, he didn't want to make it. Two Labor senators on the committee did make the case, calling on their government to increase the allowance for single people—the group suffering most under current arrangements. Single unemployed folk, need it be said, aren't part of Gillard's beloved "working families" demographic.

Newstart is now so low, says the Business Council, that it's likely to be a barrier to employment. "Trying to survive on $35 a day is likely to erode the capacity of individuals to present themselves well or maintain their readiness for work."

How do you hunt for a job if you can't afford a train fare to get to an interview? Or decent clothes? What if you don't even have a permanent address to put on a CV [curriculum vitae, or resume]? While Newstart was envisaged as temporary support, more than 60 per cent of recipients have been unemployed for more than a year. As one welfare group put it, Newstart is a pathway to poverty—not a job.

The Consequences of Low Benefits

Over the past year, I have been recording my interactions with beggars for an essay published in the latest *Meanjin*. "Why give to beggars in a welfare state?" a friend asked when I told him of the project, and it's a valid question. One answer might be because the dole is simply not enough. People beg for many reasons—opportunism, addiction, convenience, desperation—but some, it seems, are begging just to get by between meagre benefits.

Reading some of the submissions to the Senate inquiry, it's clear that for a significant minority of Australians, life has become a degrading struggle to make ends meet. More than 80 per cent of people on Newstart are renting, about half of them in the private market. Private rents are exorbitant—even if you qualify for rent assistance of up to $60 a week.

High rents drive poor people into outer suburbs, where public transport is infrequent and costly. Welfare agencies tell of a huge demand for emergency food relief, too. Then there are other costs—from the price of tobacco, for smokers, to servicing inflated short-term loans. As "Graham", a Newstart recipient, told researchers at Melbourne University, "Living on the dole is not living, it's surviving".

At Christmas, when the pressure to buy stuff reaches a secular crescendo, the struggle to keep up gets harder. One man I met on the streets told me he had used money earned selling cards to buy a Christmas present for his teenage son. When I mentioned this to a friend who works as a criminal lawyer, she said, "you'd be amazed how many of my clients steal to buy Christmas presents for their kids".

As a society, we must surely be judged on how we treat those most in need.

The Need for Higher Benefits

The Greens [Australian political party] and others want a $50-a-week boost to the single Newstart rate. (A broader, costlier reform would involve indexing the dole in a similar way to pensions.) Where might that $50 a week come from? New research by the Australian Bureau of Statistics shows the richest fifth of Australian households receive nearly half of all wages paid—and also get 12 per cent of government assistance. The second-richest fifth get 11 per cent.

Middle-class welfare is thriving in the form of the child care rebate (not income tested) and the still generous baby bonus.

The rebate is apparently aimed at helping mothers stay in jobs. This is a laudable goal. But really, whose need is greater? The family earning $130,000 a year and getting a $7500 government refund for child care? Or the unemployed person struggling to feed, clothe and house herself on a pittance?

As a society, we must surely be judged on how we treat those most in need. Means testing the child care rebate is long overdue.

The committee recommended lifting the amount that Newstart recipients can earn to the equivalent of six hours a fortnight at the minimum wage. This is great for those who can get work, but what if you can't? The committee cautioned against "increasing financial incentives" to stay on the dole—yet the dole is so low it is clearly cementing disadvantage.

Newstart, says the Business Council, "no longer meets a reasonable community standard of adequacy". Yet a Labor government—in power for five years—has kept it brutally low. What a topsy-turvy world we live in.

Periodical and Internet Sources Bibliography

The following articles have been selected to supplement the diverse views presented in this chapter.

James Ball, Dan Milmo, and Ben Ferguson	"Half of UK's Young Black Males Are Unemployed," *Guardian* (UK), March 9, 2012.
Ronald Brownstein	"Trend Lines Favor Working Women," *National Journal*, June 19, 2010.
Nancy Cook	"What Happens to the Children of the Unemployed?," *National Journal*, October 11, 2012.
Michelle FlorCruz	"Unemployment Report: China's College Graduates Struggle to Find Jobs," *International Business Times*, December 12, 2012.
Rashi Aditi Ghosh	"Unemployment Rate Is Higher Amongst Highly Educated Rural Indians," *DNA India*, September 18, 2012.
Daniel Halper	"Big Jump in Unemployment for Blacks," *Weekly Standard*, November 2, 2012.
Richard W. Johnson and Janice Park	"Unemployment Statistics on Older Americans," Urban Institute, September 7, 2012. www.urban.org.
Kunal Kumar Kundu	"Young, Jobless and Indian," *India Real Time* (blog), *Wall Street Journal*, November 23, 2012. http://blogs.wsj.com.
Jason Overdorf	"India: Rosy Unemployment Data Belies Grim Reality," GlobalPost, October 22, 2012. www.globalpost.com.

GLOBALVIEWPOINTS

CHAPTER 3

The Causes
of Unemployment

High Unemployment in the United States Is Caused by the Global Recession

Heather Boushey

In the following viewpoint, Heather Boushey argues that high unemployment in the United States is not caused by the low skills of the unemployed but rather by the housing bubble and financial crisis. Boushey claims that a lack of demand from employers and other cyclical factors explain unemployment rather than "structural" factors pertaining to facts about the unemployed. She contends that the only way to resolve the problem is to address this gap in demand. Boushey is senior economist at the Center for American Progress.

As you read, consider the following questions:

1. How many Americans were unemployed at the height of unemployment in 2010, according to Boushey?

2. What two examples of structural factors does Boushey give that she denies as the causes of unemployment?

3. Boushey recommends investments in what three examples of infrastructure as a way to enhance productivity and growth?

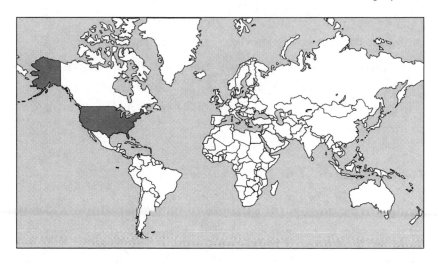

More than 12 million people in the United States are pounding the pavement, searching for a job without luck. This is fewer than a few years ago—we had a high of nearly 16 million unemployed in 2010—but far more than at any point in recent memory prior to the Great Recession.

The Driver of High Unemployment

Why are people out of work? Some economists have been arguing that today's high unemployment is explained by a mismatch between the skills that employers are looking for and the skills that the unemployed have. "Firms have jobs, but can't find appropriate workers," the Minneapolis Fed [Federal Reserve] president Narayana Kocherlakota said in Michigan in 2010. "The workers want to work, but can't find appropriate jobs." Indeed, there were 3.7 million unfilled job openings in the United States in June of this year [2012], according to the Bureau of Labor Statistics.

However, it's unlikely that this phenomenon is a major driver of persistently high unemployment. In 2007, only about five percent of people in the United States who wanted a job couldn't find one. Eighteen months later, nearly ten percent of those who wanted a job couldn't find one. Did the skills of the labor force deteriorate so demonstrably in a year and a half that millions were suddenly unemployable?

Of course not. What happened was the collapse of the housing bubble and the ensuing financial crisis, which stripped trillions in wealth from family balance sheets and sank demand for goods and services.

A Problem of Demand

Indeed, most economists agree that today's high unemployment is "cyclical." That is, we agree that most people are out of work because of the recession and its lingering effects on the labor market, not because there is something wrong with the unemployed.

For example, the *New York Times'* Binyamin Appelbaum reported from the annual conference of the Federal Reserve Board last August that "pretty much everyone here is upset about the breakdown of fiscal policy, which is becoming a principal drag on growth." Demand and cyclical factors explain unemployment, rather than what economists might call "structural" factors, such as a lack among the unemployed of adequate skills or incentives to find a job.

Most people are out of work because of the recession and its lingering effects on the labor market.

Given that the problem of unemployment is not the fault of the unemployed but rather insufficient demand for their labor, solutions should address that macroeconomic root cause. While it is always important to make sure that workers—and especially low-wage workers and young people—have access to the education and training that they need to make the most of their career, investments in workforce development will not be enough to solve today's unemployment problem. If

The Skills Mismatch Theory of Unemployment

This "skills mismatch" is routinely held up to explain why the unemployment rate is still at 8.2% . . . and why nearly half of those out of work have been so for more than six months. . . .

In recent months, researchers . . . have expressed skepticism about the existence of a national skills mismatch. A larger body of work, stretching back decades, paints a murky picture about how broad based a problem worker skill level is. Despite this, policy makers have fretted about the issue for 30 years, in periods of high unemployment and low.

Barbara Kiviat, "The Big Jobs Myth: American Workers Aren't Ready for American Jobs," Atlantic, July 25, 2012.

the unemployment rate was half what it was today, then education and job training could push it down even further. But that's not where we are.

The Solution to the Problem

To solve the jobs problem, we need to find a way to make up for the gap in demand that continues to plague the U.S. economy. Because this recession was caused by the collapse of a still struggling housing market, we cannot expect our recovery to be driven—as is typical—by an increase in housing purchases.

And we need to ensure that the mistakes of the past that destabilized our economy are not repeated. Among other things, an important way to make sure that we have stable growth moving forward is to make sure that the financial sector focuses on its true value to our economy, which is making capital available for productive investment and realigning the growth in wages with the growth in productivity. For decades, U.S. workers have produced more goods and services for each hour of work. But their pay has not risen commensurately, which has contributed to the instability in demand. Indeed, income inequality has increased, requiring a growing share of the middle class to pile on debt just to make ends meet. That's not a sustainable jobs plan.

We need to find a way to make up for the gap in demand that continues to plague the U.S. economy.

A good way forward in the short term would be for policy makers to make the kinds of investments that will enhance productivity and growth in the years to come but will get people back to work now. Investments in our nation's roads and bridges, school upgrades and new construction, and fixing our nation's energy grid are all good ideas for right now. (The Center for American Progress estimates that the U.S. needs to spend, at a minimum, an additional $129.2 billion a year over the next decade to keep pace with the country's infrastructure needs—a level of investment that could produce over two million new jobs.) We also should focus on stemming the tide of job losses among schoolteachers and public safety officers and, instead, put them back to work educating the next generation and keeping our communities safe.

Unemployment in Europe Is the Result of the Welfare State

James M. Roberts and J.D. Foster

In the following viewpoint, James M. Roberts and J.D. Foster argue that the failure of monetary policy and high social welfare spending in Europe are causing economic collapse in several countries. The authors fault generous welfare spending with a host of problems, including unemployment and high debt. Roberts is a research fellow for economic freedom and growth in the Center for International Trade and Economics, and Foster is Norman B. Ture Senior Fellow in the Economics of Fiscal Policy in the Thomas A. Roe Institute for Economic Policy Studies, both at the Heritage Foundation.

As you read, consider the following questions:

1. According to the authors, what five European countries suffering from economic collapse are known as the PIIGS?

2. Roberts and Foster claim that the European welfare state and welfare payments have led to what perception about the status of unemployment?

3. The authors caution that the United States is on track to spend what fraction of the economy on entitlements in a couple decades?

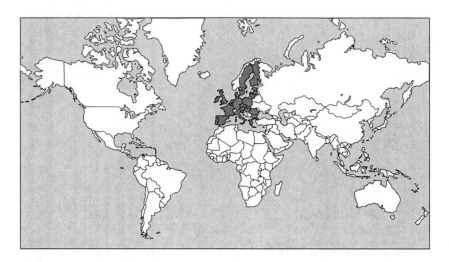

Europe's socialist (or "social democratic") welfare state is collapsing under the load of unsustainable debt. There is no chance European politicians will ever make good on the many costly and unfunded entitlements they have promised their citizens.

A Crisis in the European Union

The fundamental problem in the European Union [EU] is a monetary policy failure. In conjunction with the debilitating effects of the social welfare state, this has led to a broad economic collapse among the lesser states—notably the PIIGS (Portugal, Ireland, Italy, Greece, and Spain), but also some of the EU's newer members—and it threatens to envelop the greater states.

For years, this collapse among the lesser states was disguised by debt accumulation—countries would borrow (at de facto concessionary interest rates) to overcome their inability to generate adequate income by producing and selling. The lack of actual and prospective growth combined with growing debt burdens has led to a long-term solvency crisis, which has been bubbling up of late into a series of liquidity crises.

The monetary and fiscal situation in the EU is increasingly unmanageable, as the debt burdens grow and growth prospects diminish further. To paraphrase an old saying: You can fool some of the credit markets all the time, and all the markets some of the time, but you cannot fool all the credit markets indefinitely.

A Rise in Instability

The vision of a "euro zone" was ill-conceived from the start. It is now increasingly acknowledged that Brussels' lack of control over social spending, especially in the PIIGS, doomed it from the beginning. Agreements (e.g., the Maastricht Treaty) to stay within EU member government spending targets were routinely flouted, even by the largest EU countries.

But the growing gap in competitiveness amongst EU members was far more important. Some, like Germany, tended to adopt policies like labor market reforms that built on their inherent economic strengths. The strong got stronger, while others, like Italy and Greece, stood still or even retreated on policies that would have sustained their international competitiveness. The focus today on shifting painfully to policies that can make these countries competitive is simply too little, too late.

For decades now, one of the most tragic costs of the European welfare state has been Europe's structural unemployment.

And now, the instability is rapidly spreading to the pillars of Europe—first Spain, then Italy, and now apparently to France. Southern Europeans kept borrowing in low-interest-rate euros (which simultaneously inflated housing bubbles in their countries) until, in [then British member of Parliament] Margaret Thatcher's words, their socialist governments "ran out of other peoples' money!" As a result, some of Europe's large private banks now hold toxic quantities of sovereign debt issued by the PIIGS and are threatened with extinction through serial defaults—thus they are deemed "too big to fail." Already there is growing worry over the solvency of France's Société Générale bank because of this crisis, with several other major European banks likely to be in trouble if the situation is not resolved.

Social Results of the Welfare State

For decades now, one of the most tragic costs of the European welfare state has been Europe's structural unemployment, especially among the young, combined with welfare payments that turned unemployment into an acceptable—even desirable—status, while stripping those affected of their dignity and sense of responsibility. The recent riots in the U.K. [United Kingdom] are an ominous reflection of this failure.

One of the key questions now is: How much longer will workers and taxpayers in Germany and other relatively more fiscally prudent countries in northern Europe be willing to work into their late 60s to subsidize (via euro zone bailouts and managed defaults) their neighbors in southern Europe so that the latter can retire early in their 50s on generous state-funded pensions and go to the beach?

The euro elites' response to date has been to try to address the solvency crisis through fiscal policy, and the liquidity crisis through additional debt—ignoring the EU's monetary policy failure because they have no politically acceptable solution. It is obvious where this will lead, as Heritage Foundation analysis has noted in the past.

Maybe, instead, some of the PIIGS will decide to exit the euro. Or perhaps the northerners will leave the euro (and the euro-denominated sovereign debts of the PIIGS) behind and resuscitate the Deutschmark? One path or the other appears inevitable.

The European social welfare state has contributed mightily to this situation by making all of Europe less competitive relative to the rest of the world, which is why the U.K., though not subject to the monetary policy failure, cannot escape the growth consequences entirely. Meanwhile, Germany's inherent strengths have allowed it to take advantage of its euro-linked trading partners.

> *For the U.S., Europe is the ultimate object lesson—a warning of what happens when government is allowed to run wild, with the resulting loss of liberty and fiscal deficits.*

The Underlying Policy Failure

Lest there be any doubt, the underlying monetary policy failure is the euro. It is now quite clear that this policy was doomed, not solely because Europe failed to harmonize it

117

with other policies, but because monetary union between fast-growth states and slow-growth states can only end in tragic monetary disintegration. The hope that it would cause slow-growth states to catch up was a pipe dream.

Will Europe's elites succeed in making one more try to save the euro zone, perhaps by creating a central EU treasury that alone has the power to issue new debt for EU countries? This would guarantee that the PIIGS pay lower interest rates than their credit histories would mandate, while the north pays more.

French president Nicolas Sarkozy reportedly aims "to seize the Greek crisis to make a quantum leap in euro zone governance." The recent assertion by Berlin and Paris that a new eurobond is dead on arrival, however, suggests Germany's patience has just about run out—apparently, that quantum leap will have to be in a different direction.

For the U.S., Europe is the ultimate object lesson—a warning of what happens when government is allowed to run wild, with the resulting loss of liberty and fiscal deficits. Fortunately, though the United States has a single currency, it largely achieved the necessary conditions for such an arrangement to be successful long ago.

The Future of the Euro

It is almost certain that this crisis will produce something new out of Europe. The emergence, whether collectively or individually, of stronger European societies with durable financial and monetary regimes would certainly be in the best interest of the U.S. and the rest of the world.

As Ambrose Evans-Pritchard reports in the *Telegraph* (U.K.), the likely short-term outcome is described by Daniel Gros from the Centre for European Policy Studies: "Germany and the other AAA states must agree to some sort of euro-bond regime. Otherwise the euro will implode." However, as noted above, France, and especially Germany, have been stoutly opposed to a eurobond, and for very good reasons. Assuming Gros is correct in his assessment, and he most likely is, the future of the euro is bleak indeed.

Meanwhile, spending by the U.S. government—presently on track to consume one-third of the economy by the time today's newborns graduate from college—must be reduced. Entitlements must be reined in and reformed; non-defense discretionary spending must be rolled back to 2008 levels.

To reduce federal spending and prevent economic collapse, U.S. policy makers should follow the Heritage Foundation's plan in "Saving the American Dream."

Unemployment in the United Kingdom Is Not Caused by a Culture of Worklessness

Tracy Shildrick, Robert MacDonald, Andy Furlong, Johann Roden, and Robert Crow

In the following viewpoint, Tracy Shildrick, Robert MacDonald, Andy Furlong, Johann Roden, and Robert Crow argue that the theory that unemployment is caused by a cultural norm passed down through generations—a culture of worklessness—is unfounded. The authors argue that there are few families in which several generations have not worked and that among families with high unemployment, a variety of other factors other than culture explain prolonged worklessness. Shildrick and MacDonald are professors of sociology at Teesside University. Furlong is professor of social inclusion and education at the University of Glasgow. Roden is a researcher. Crow is a research associate in the Social Futures Institute of Teesside University.

As you read, consider the following questions:

1. The authors claim that statistics suggest that the proportion of workless households of two generations make up what percentage of workless households?

Adapted from *Are 'Cultures of Worklessness' Passed Down the Generations?*, by Tracy Shildrick, Robert MacDonald, Andy Furlong, Johann Roden, and Robert Crow, published in 2012 by the Joseph Rowntree Foundation. Reproduced by permission of the Joseph Rowntree Foundation.

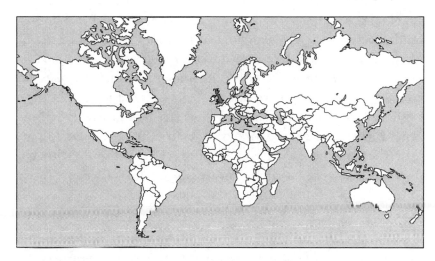

2. The authors estimate that there are how many families in the United Kingdom in which two generations have never worked?

3. Theories about cultures of worklessness suggest people are unemployed because of what, according to the authors?

The idea that worklessness can be explained, at least in part, by the familial inheritance of values and practices that discourage employment and encourage welfare dependency, is a powerful one. Indeed, much UK [United Kingdom] policy thinking continues to be based on the premise that workless people can become dependent on welfare and that this dependence is passed on between different generations within families, particularly in neighbourhoods where high rates of worklessness prevail. Through a critical case-study approach, using methods and research sites most likely to reveal 'intergenerational cultures of worklessness', the project put these ideas to the test.

Finding Workless Households

Social statistics suggest that the proportion of workless households with two generations who have never worked is very small—approximately half of one per cent of workless house-holds. Despite dogged searching in localities with high rates of worklessness across decades we were *unable to locate any families in which there were three generations in which no one had ever worked.* Although we know of no other studies that have explicitly sought to measure or research families where 'three generations have never worked', if such families do exist, logically they will be even fewer in number than those estimated to have two-generational worklessness (i.e., an even more miniscule fraction of workless families).

The idea that worklessness can be explained, at least in part, by the familial inheritance of values and practices that discourage employment and encourage welfare dependency, is a powerful one.

Eventually, we recruited twenty families where there was:

- a parent in the middle generation (aged between late 30s and mid-50s) who had experienced very long-term worklessness (defined as currently being out of work and having been so for at least the last 5 years—although many had been out of work for longer than this)

- at least one child of working age (typically aged 16 to mid-20s) who was unemployed (most of whom had never had a job).

The difficulties in recruiting this sample, and the need to relax our initial recruitment criteria to do so, corroborate available statistical evidence showing long-term, cross-generational worklessness in households to be a rare phenomenon.

Explanations for Worklessness

The typical story for the majority in this middle generation was of leaving school and entering employment relatively easily. Despite this early engagement with the labour market, when interviewed, these mid-aged interviewees all had long histories of worklessness. We met two people in the middle generation who had never had a job (recent research tells us that there are no more than 20,230 families in the UK where two generations have never worked).

Rarely were there simple explanations for why individuals in the middle generation had such extensive records of worklessness. Typically, a range of problems associated with social exclusion and poverty combined to distance people from the labour market. These problems included, but were not limited to:

- poor schooling and educational underachievement

- problematic drug and alcohol use

- the attraction of opportunities in illicit economies (such as drug dealing) when legitimate opportunities were scarce

- criminal victimisation

- offending and imprisonment

- domestic violence, and family and housing instability

- physical and mental ill health.

Children of those with extensive worklessness in this middle generation comprised the younger generation of the sample (and were typically aged 16 to their mid-20s). Most of the younger generation had never been employed. Whilst emphatically not occupying 'a culture of worklessness', they carried the disadvantages of being brought up in largely workless households with multiple problems (such as having spent time in local authority care, having faced housing moves that disrupted their education, and lacking the family social and cultural capital that can help people into jobs). Nevertheless, they clung to conventional values and aspirations about jobs.

Members of their wider family and social networks who were in employment acted as role models and sources of inspiration to these young people. The main explanation for their worklessness was that they were attempting to make their transitions into the labour market in a period of national economic downturn, and of high national and very high rates of local unemployment.

Rarely were there simple explanations for why individuals in the middle generation had such extensive records of worklessness.

The So-Called Culture of Worklessness

Theories about cultures of worklessness suggest that people are unemployed because of their values, attitudes and behaviours rather than because of a shortage of jobs. In simple terms, they imply people prefer a life on welfare benefits to working for a living. A theory of 'intergenerational cultures of worklessness' adds to this by arguing that such values, behaviours and attitudes are transmitted in families, from unemployed parents to their children who, in turn, pass on anti-employment and pro-welfare dependency attitudes to their own children. Over time, these cultures of worklessness become entrenched and are said to explain the persistent, concentrated worklessness that can be found in some British towns and cities.

We found no evidence to support the idea that participants were part of a culture of worklessness, and none for the idea of intergenerational cultures of worklessness. Despite their long-term worklessness, parents actively strove for better for their children and often assisted them in searching for jobs. Young people in these families described wanting to avoid the poverty, worklessness and other problems that had affected their parents. Running directly counter to theories of intergenerational cultures of worklessness, the research found

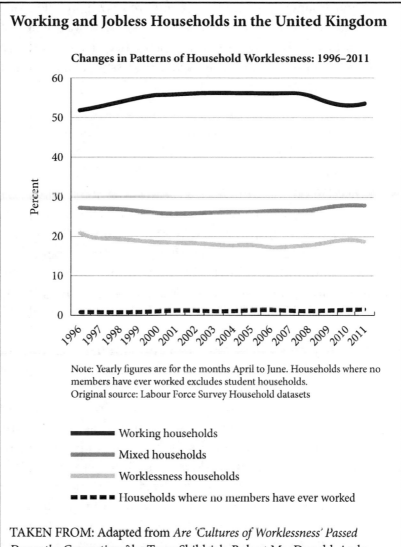

Working and Jobless Households in the United Kingdom

Changes in Patterns of Household Worklessness: 1996–2011

Note: Yearly figures are for the months April to June. Households where no members have ever worked excludes student households.
Original source: Labour Force Survey Household datasets

———— Working households

———— Mixed households

———— Worklessness households

■ ■ ■ ■ ■ Households where no members have ever worked

TAKEN FROM: Adapted from *Are 'Cultures of Worklessness' Passed Down the Generations?* by Tracy Shildrick, Robert MacDonald, Andy Furlong, Johann Roden and Robert Crow, published in 2012 by the Joseph Rowntree Foundation. Reproduced by permission of the Joseph Rowntree Foundation.

that conventional, mainstream attitudes to and values about work were widespread in both the middle and younger generations. Employment was understood to offer social, psychological and financial advantages (compared with worklessness and a reliance on benefits). Interviewees knew it was better to be in work than to be out of work, partly because of the deep and long-term poverty that extensive worklessness had brought to these families.

The notion of three or even two generations of families where no one has ever worked is ill-founded as an explanation for contemporary worklessness in the UK.

The interviewees did not occupy social or family networks that were isolated from employment or from working cultures. Inevitably, given the localities we studied, unemployment was common in their family and social networks—but, so was employment. Even in the very deprived neighbourhoods we studied, most working-age residents were in jobs. A telling finding (against the cultures of worklessness thesis) was the variability of work histories in the families we studied. Employed family members (e.g., other siblings or members of the extended family) sometimes served as role models or provided inspiration, especially to younger interviewees. We found very little evidence of people working fraudulently, 'on the side' whilst in receipt of benefits, which is claimed to be another facet of cultures of worklessness. Many in the sample did 'work', however, if we use the term to mean something more than paid employment. The work of looking after children in very difficult circumstances and caring for other relatives, meant that some women (and it was women rather than men in the main) were limited in their opportunities to engage with employment. Volunteering was not uncommon in the sample; for people with limited labour market opportunities voluntary work has been found to provide some of the positive social and psychological benefits of employment. Finally, some individuals became involved with criminal work, particularly shoplifting and drug dealing, usually to fund their own dependent drug use.

A Failed Explanation for Worklessness

The study concludes that the notion of three or even two generations of families where no one has ever worked is ill-founded as an explanation for contemporary worklessness in the UK. Such families account for a vanishingly small fraction of the workless. Our research shows that the more general idea of 'intergenerational cultures of worklessness' is also an unhelpful concept in trying to understand patterns of extensive worklessness in families.

We would stress that the sample of families in our study is extremely unusual. Their histories of very lengthy worklessness are typical neither of working-class people in Glasgow and Teesside, nor of other people living in poverty and experiencing worklessness. Other research has shown that a pattern of churning between low-paid jobs and unemployment is likely to be a more common experience. What makes them unusual and explains their distance from the labour market is the sheer preponderance of hardships and problems in their lives. The report concludes that politicians and policy makers should abandon the idea of intergenerational cultures of worklessness—and, indeed, of cultures of worklessness. These ideas failed to explain even the extreme cases of prolonged worklessness we uncovered so they are unlikely to capture more common and widespread experiences of worklessness.

Youth Unemployment in the Middle East and North Africa Has a Variety of Causes

Masood Ahmed, Dominique Guillaume, and Davide Furceri

In the following viewpoint, Masood Ahmed, Dominique Guillaume, and Davide Furceri argue that the high levels of youth unemployment that exist in the oil-importing countries of the Middle East and North Africa are caused by demographic changes, skill mismatches, labor market policies, and high-paid public sector jobs. They conclude that there is a need to change structural policies and make investments in job creation. Ahmed is director of the Middle East and Central Asia Department, Guillaume a deputy division chief, and Furceri an economist at the International Monetary Fund.

As you read, consider the following questions:

1. According to the authors, approximately what fraction of youth in the Middle East and North Africa (MENA) are unemployed?

2. How much higher are public sector wages than private sector wages in MENA, according to the authors?

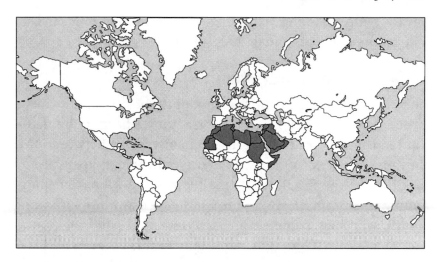

3. MENA oil-importing nations will need to add approximately how many full-time positions over the next decade to absorb the unemployed and new workers, according to the authors?

Addressing high unemployment is a long-standing but increasingly urgent challenge for MENA [Middle East and North Africa] oil-importing countries [Djibouti, Egypt, Jordan, Lebanon, Mauritania, Morocco, Syria, and Tunisia]. Unemployment in the MENA region is the highest in the world and largely a youth phenomenon. The share of youth (ages 15 to 24) in total unemployment at least doubles the total rate. Moreover, at about 25%, the youth unemployment rate in the MENA exceeds that of any other region in the world—a rate that reaches up to about 30% in Tunisia. The recent social and political events in the region have contributed to a decline in economic activity and to increased unemployment. In 2011, unemployment has increased in the MENA countries, with the largest increase registered for Tunisia (about 7 percentage points) and Egypt (about 3.5 percentage points).

Unusually, education in this region is not a guarantee against unemployment. In fact, unemployment tends to increase with schooling, exceeding 15% for those with tertiary education in Egypt, Jordan and Tunisia.

A Demographic Transition

In most regions of the world, the duration of unemployment spells is shorter for youth than for adults, reflecting the natural tendency of youth to more frequently move between jobs. In most MENA countries, however, youth unemployment appears to be the result of waiting for the right job. Thus, unemployment spells may be longer, especially for educated youth, who may require more time to find a good job match for their skills. This is an important point, because it is the duration of unemployment, rather than its occurrence, that is most detrimental to human capital accumulation.

Unemployment in the MENA region is the highest in the world and largely a youth phenomenon.

High labour force growth, skill mismatches, labour and product market rigidities, large public sectors, and high reservation wages have been key factors behind the large and persistent level of youth unemployment.

Demographic pressures in MENA might be a leading cause of the high youth unemployment rates in the region. The origins of the current demographic trends began in the 1950s. Over the past 50 years, MENA countries experienced large declines in infant mortality rates. The combination of low infant mortality rates and high fertility rates between 1950 and 1980 led to high population growth rates, which translated into high labour force growth rates from 1970 through 2000 and beyond.

Over the past decade, the labour force in MENA has grown at an average annual rate of 2.7%, faster than in any other region of the world, save Africa. And it will continue to outpace most other regions. The number of labour force entrants remains daunting—approximately 10.7 million new entrants are expected to join the labour force in the coming decade, compared with 10.2 million in the previous decade. However, youth labour force growth is expected to gradually decelerate over the next decade, easing labour market supply. And in some countries, such as Tunisia, the demographic transition will occur even earlier.

Education and Hiring Practices

Labour market mismatches have been driven by the inability of the economy to create highly skilled work but also by the inappropriate content and delivery of education. Over the past decades, the MENA countries have made important strides in providing education. Average years of schooling (for those 15 years and older) increased fourfold between 1960 and 2000, more than any other region in the world. In 1999, average years of schooling in MENA was 5.3 years, ahead of South Asia (4.6 years) and sub-Saharan Africa (3.5 years), and only one year behind East Asia (6.6 years) and Latin America and the Caribbean (6.4 years). With respect to illiteracy rates, however, the MENA region still lags behind other regions of the world. In addition, entrepreneurs regularly cite the lack of suitable skills as an important constraint to hiring and unemployment rates are highest among the most educated. Taken together, this suggests that education systems in the region fail to produce graduates with needed skills.

According to *The Global Competitiveness Report 2011–2012*, hiring and firing regulations in most MENA countries are more restrictive than those in the average emerging and developing country. Similarly, data from enterprise surveys indicates that, worldwide, the percentage of firms identifying labour regulation as a major constraint to their business operations is, on average, greatest in MENA. In addition, indicators of labour market flexibility show that such rigidities are particularly high in MENA and could significantly limit employment creation, particularly for first-time job seekers, by discouraging firms from expanding employment in response to favourable changes in the economic climate.

The MENA region also has the highest central government wage bill in the world (as a percentage of GDP [gross domestic product])—9.8% of GDP compared to a global average of 5.4%. The high wage bill partly reflects the fact that government employment in MENA is comparatively high, but it also reflects the fact that public sector wages in MENA were on average 30% higher than private sector wages, compared to 20% *lower* worldwide. Around the turn of this century, the public sector accounted for about one-third of total employment in Syria, 22% in Tunisia, and about 35% in Jordan and Egypt.

Education systems in the region fail to produce graduates with needed skills.

The Public Sector

Public sector employment shares are even higher as a percentage of nonagricultural employment—reaching 42% in Jordan and 70% in Egypt. The dominant role of the public sector as employer throughout MENA has distorted labour market outcomes and diverted resources away from a potentially more dynamic private sector. Government hiring practices have typically inflated wage expectations and placed a premium on diplomas over actual skills, influencing educational choices and contributing to skill mismatches.

The comparatively greater job security, higher wages, and more generous on-wage benefits offered by the public sector have inflated wage expectations among new entrants. In fact, public sector wages are 48% and 36% higher than those offered by the private sector in Egypt and Tunisia, respectively. Relatively high wages and benefits encourage workers to seek jobs in the public sector instead of potentially more productive jobs in the private sector.

In addition, generous child care and maternity leave policies encourage females to focus on obtaining public sector jobs. However, public sector jobs remain valued because of job security, high compensation and benefits, and lack of opportunities in the private sector. It appears that the system essentially has created a dual labour market, with the public sector representing the high-wage, high-benefit sector.

The Need to Increase Employment

To absorb the unemployed and new entrants to the labour force, the MENA oil importers will need to increase employment by an estimated 18.5 million full-time positions over the next decade—although even this would leave the ratio of employment to working-age population lower than that currently observed in any other region.

Reaching the job target will require a combination of permanently higher economic growth and reforms to improve the responsiveness of the labour market. The fact that youth unemployment has remained high for so long indicates that the problem is largely structural and will not be resolved by a cyclical increase in output, but would need a sustained high and job-creating growth, supported by a sound macroeconomic environment.

A higher growth performance will be necessary but not sufficient to significantly reduce unemployment over the medium term. In particular, in the absence of structural reforms aimed at improving the responsiveness of labour market conditions to changes in economic activity, higher economic growth is likely to have only a modest impact on youth unemployment. In this context, deepening structural policies such as:

- *Improving the flexibility of the labour market* will be essential to increase labour demand over the medium term and to facilitate the integration of young out-

Youth Unemployment by World Region, 2010

Based on data from the International Labour Organization and International Monetary Fund.

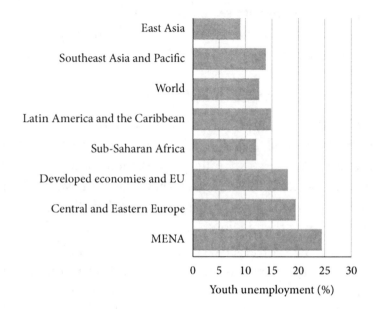

TAKEN FROM: Masood Ahmed, Dominique Guillaume, and Davide Furceri, "Youth Unemployment in the MENA Region: Determinants and Challenges," *Addressing the 100 Million Youth Challenge: Perspectives on Youth Employment in the Arab World in 2012*, World Economic Forum, 2012.

sider workers into the labour market. In this context, reforms aimed at reducing search and hiring costs will be crucial.

- *Improving the business climate and fostering product market competition* will also be key to reducing unemployment over the medium term. In particular, lower barriers to entry curb market power and incumbents' rents, and they tend to reduce wage claims and close the gap between productivity and real wages. Moreover, stronger competition may reduce bargaining positions of employers and increase employment costs for higher wages. Reduced rent sharing would also decrease the time spent searching for employment opportunities in high-wage sectors. In addition, improvement in business climate and product market competition will also be essential to raising potential growth over the medium term.

- *Addressing skill mismatches* will be key to reducing youth unemployment. In this context, realigning curricula with private sector needs, reforming university admission policies and improving the quality of educational systems will be of crucial importance.

- *Improving public sector hiring practices and compensation policies.* Public sector hiring procedures should place greater emphasis on skills and competition and less on paper qualifications. Moreover, strengthening the link between compensation and performance and implementing merit-based promotion policies would also send the right signals regarding skill formation for young people.

- *Reducing the size of public sector.* Large government sectors tend to crowd out private investment and to reduce the size of the private sector and sustained growth over the medium term. In addition, large government sectors often involve higher taxes, which can have depressive effects on aggregate demand and on the labour market.

The Need for Investment and New Policies

The ongoing social and political turmoil in the region has created urgency to start implementing measures in the short term that would also have long-term benefits.

Investment in infrastructure can have a sizable impact on employment generation, even in the short term. For example, evidence from Latin America and the Caribbean suggests that about 40,000 annual direct and indirect new jobs can be created in the short term for every US$1 billion spent on infrastructure projects. Extrapolating these numbers to Egypt and Tunisia, for instance, suggests that 1% of GDP spent on infrastructure could generate in the short term as many as 87,000 new jobs in Egypt and 18,000 jobs in Tunisia. To have an immediate effect, policy makers in the region can therefore seek to bring forward viable labour-intensive infrastructure projects that are already in the pipeline, while maintaining fiscal sustainability. Such a policy will not only provide wage employment—including for young people—but will also enhance long-term growth, thereby leading to sustained job creation.

A higher growth performance will be necessary but not sufficient to significantly reduce unemployment over the medium term.

To encourage job creation, policy makers can explore the possibility of giving tax incentives or providing credit guarantees to viable labour-intensive small and medium enterprises, as was done in many emerging markets and transition economies during the global financial crisis. Moreover, removing impediments to access to credit would also help these enterprises.

The Need for Effective Training Programs

The region offers a growing range of promising youth-oriented training programmes. One such example is the Education for Employment Foundation (EFE), which currently operates in several countries in the region, including Egypt, Jordan and Morocco. EFE works with corporations and industries to assess demand for skills and to provide corresponding tailored training programmes for young people. Through both in-class and on-the-job training, EFE has proven successful in providing job seekers with skills relevant to businesses and placing unemployed youth in jobs. For example, 85% of programme graduates were placed in jobs in Jordan and 86% were placed in jobs and internships in Morocco. Policy makers should seek to scale up and replicate such promising programmes.

Given the magnitude of youth unemployment and the urgent need to address it, policy makers may want to initiate new investments in well-designed training programmes, in addition to expanding training programmes that have shown some success. It is crucial that policy makers act now, given that it may take some time to reap the benefits of new investments. Some lessons can be learned from the experiences of other countries when designing such programmes. For example, evaluations of youth training programmes in Latin America indicate that those that are demand driven, offer on-the-job training, focus on both hard- and soft-skill formation, monitor performance and perform impact evaluations have a significant positive impact on employment and earnings of programme participants.

Given the magnitude of youth unemployment and the urgent need to address it, policy makers may want to initiate new investments in well-designed training programmes.

At the same time, when designing short-term solutions to youth unemployment, governments should ensure that such solutions do not harm the long-term goal of sustainable job creation and productive skill formation. For example, in light of the ongoing political turmoil and uncertainty, governments may be enticed to quickly create unneeded jobs in the already large public sector. Such a policy, which may be difficult to unwind later, may distort labour market incentives and divert resources away from a potentially more vibrant private sector. As another example, giving subsidies to the educated unemployed youth, while well intended and providing relief, may reinforce skills mismatches for future labour market entrants if the qualification for such subsidies is based solely on diplomas and credentials.

In sum, the key to successfully addressing the formidable youth unemployment challenge in MENA oil-importing countries is to turn the large and growing labour force into an asset, rather than a constraint. This will require ensuring sustained, high, and job-intensive growth; refocusing education and training to reduce skills mismatches; enhancing labour market flexibility and maintaining macroeconomic stability.

In South Korea, Overeducation Has Aggravated Unemployment

Christian Oliver and Kang Buseong

In the following viewpoint, Christian Oliver and Kang Buseong argue that South Korea's passion for education has actually become a drain on the economy. Oliver and Buseong claim that high unemployment among youth is partly due to the youth being educated for the wrong jobs. They argue that an overabundance of college graduates is ill-equipped to fill the necessary employment needs in manual jobs and at smaller employers. Oliver is Korea correspondent at Financial Times, *and Buseong is a reporter in Seoul, South Korea.*

As you read, consider the following questions:

1. According to the authors, how many colleges and universities are there in South Korea?

2. What percentage of unemployed men and what percentage of unemployed women have attended college or university, according to the authors?

3. The authors claim that between 1995 and 2010, the number of Koreans attending vocational school dropped by what fraction?

Christian Oliver and Kang Buseong, "S Korea Faces Problem of 'Over-Education,'" *Financial Times* (UK), June 11, 2010. Reproduced by permission.

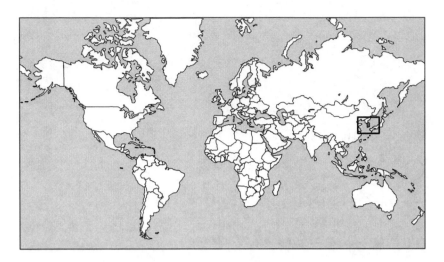

South Korea has some of the world's most over-educated bakers. In one class in Seoul teaching muffin and scone making, there are graduates in Russian, fine art and animation. For South Korean parents, the world's highest spenders on their children's education, something is going horribly wrong.

"I wanted to ease the burden on my parents by earning just a little something and finding a job that could give me something more dependable than temporary work," said one 29-year-old trainee baker. Since graduating in art she could only find part-time work as a waitress. Like so many young people asked about finding work in a socially competitive society where unemployment is a stigma, she was too embarrassed to give her name.

A Passion for Education

South Koreans often attribute their economic success to a passion for education. But the country of 48m has overdone it, with 407 colleges and universities churning out an over-abundance of graduates.

Over-education has become a crippling financial drain on Asia's fourth biggest economy. South Korean families mire themselves in debt and burn more than 3 per cent of gross domestic product on night schools and crammers dedicated exclusively to passing formulaic university entrance examinations.

After all that effort, Koreans joke they have simply created *Itaebaek*, meaning "mostly unemployed 20-somethings".

The Problem of Youth Unemployment

"Reckless university enrolment has aggravated both the private education burden and youth unemployment. It's a huge loss, not just for households but the whole country," said Lee Myung-bak, the president, who is trying to combat 82 per cent enrolment in tertiary education by strengthening vocational schools.

While unemployment among the over-30s averages between 3 and 4 per cent, it runs at 10 per cent among the under-30s. These headline figures disguise the number of graduates in dead-end temporary jobs. Some 34 per cent of unemployed men and 43 per cent of jobless women have attended college or university.

Over-education has become a crippling financial drain on Asia's fourth biggest economy.

The plethora of graduates also causes shortfalls in the manual labour sector, triggering a wave of low-skilled immigrant workers—mainly from China, Mongolia and Southeast Asia—who now constitute more than 1 per cent of the population.

"The grave problem in Korea is that families fundamentally believe that education will be a way to climb the ladder. So even poor families spurn anything in manual labour and pay huge amounts for education, taking on big loans," said

141

Kim Young-gyoung, president of the youth community union, a group dedicated to helping young people integrate into the workplace.

Job Growth in South Korea

The government has put unemployment high on its list of priorities but flagship public works programmes are of no interest to educated youngsters. In late 2008, the government announced river damming and dredging projects intended to create 230,000 jobs by 2012. With 8 per cent of the work done, the schemes have only created 5,000 jobs.

"Most of the members of the youth union think the money being put into the river projects would be better invested expanding opportunities at small- and medium-sized companies," Ms Kim said.

South Korea's economy is still dominated by massive conglomerates called *chaebol* which have intensely competitive graduate recruitment with high drop-out rates. Beneath that, middle-sized companies are far less adept at integrating university leavers.

Graduates are hitting problems while overall prognoses for South Korean employment are healthy. Tim Condon, Asia economist at ING, predicts Korea will create 15,000 to 20,000 jobs each month. Barclays Capital agreed the job outlook was bright but cautioned unemployment among the under-30s was a weakness that could undermine the "quality of growth".

Fixing Vocational Education

The Organisation for Economic Co-operation and Development [OECD] last year [2009] identified major flaws in South Korea's vocational education. In 1995, half of Koreans attended vocational high schools but the number has now dropped to about a quarter. Those at vocational schools receive a very academic education from teachers with little knowledge of the workplace, the OECD says.

The OECD also called on industry to play a more constructive role in vocational qualifications, saying students were often used for repetitive drudgery by local companies rather than being taught useful skills.

To combat these weaknesses in the system, South Korea has launched "Meister schools" hoping to train master craftsmen in the German model. Under a pilot scheme, there are 21 such schools, increasing to 50 by 2012.

"We can show that even if people do not go to university, they can still be successful in the job market," said Kim Chong-yeon, an employment expert at the education ministry.

High-spending parents have yet to be convinced.

Periodical and Internet Sources Bibliography

The following articles have been selected to supplement the diverse views presented in this chapter.

Steven A. Camarota	"The Employment Picture for Less-Educated Workers," Center for Immigration Studies, December 2012. www.cis.org.
Tyler Cowen and Jayme Lemke	"10 Percent Unemployment Forever?," *Foreign Policy*, January 5, 2011.
Diana Furchtgott-Roth	"How Obamacare Increases Unemployment," Manhattan Institute for Policy Research, March 2012. www.manhattan-institute.org.
Luke Holland	"How Austerity Is Eroding Human Rights," Al Jazeera, June 27, 2012. www.aljazeera.com.
IRIN	"Sri Lanka: Legacy of War—Unemployment and Homelessness," May 21, 2012. www.irinnews.org.
Robert MacDonald and Tracy Shildrick	"Exposed: The Myth of a 'Culture of Worklessness,'" *Guardian* (UK), December 14, 2012.
Ramesh Ponnuru	"Unemployment in Red and Blue," *National Review Online*, August 17, 2012. www.nationalreview.com.
Anthony Randazzo	"High Unemployment the New Normal," Reason.com, May 10, 2012.
Gita Subrahmanyam	"Tackling Youth Unemployment in the Maghreb," African Development Bank, *Economic Brief*, 2011. www.afdb.org.
Helen Warrell	"Report Finds Immigration Link to Unemployment," *Financial Times* (UK), January 10, 2012.

GLOBALVIEWPOINTS

CHAPTER 4

The Solutions to Unemployment

Stimulus Spending in the United States Has Lessened Unemployment

Michael Greenstone and Adam Looney

In the following viewpoint, Michael Greenstone and Adam Looney argue that recent evidence supports the view that states that increased expenditures the most in the wake of the Great Recession had smaller increases in unemployment than states that spent less. Greenstone and Looney argue that federal stimulus spending allowed states to increase expenditures and, thus, can be credited with boosting employment. Greenstone is director and Looney is policy director of the Hamilton Project; they are both senior fellows in economic studies at the Brookings Institution.

As you read, consider the following questions:

1. The authors examine two new studies on the impact of what government-spending bill?

2. The unemployment rate in the United States increased by how many percentage points between 2007 and 2010, according to the authors?

3. According to the authors, if the economy adds about 208,000 jobs per month, in what year will the "jobs gap" close?

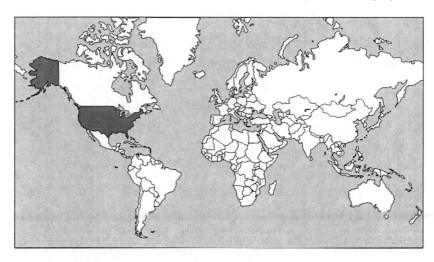

The labor market continued its modest rate of expansion in June, according to today's [July 6, 2012's] employment report. Employers added 80,000 jobs last month, about the number required simply to keep up with growth in the labor force. And the unemployment rate was unchanged at 8.2 percent. Most other indicators of labor market activity showed little movement—the employment-to-population ratio, the number of long-term unemployed, and the number of persons employed part-time because they were unable to find full-time work remained essentially unchanged. All told, today's employment report seems to confirm a slowing in the pace of recovery over the last three months from the solid pace set at the start of the year.

The Impact of Government Stimulus Spending

The Great Recession has profoundly affected almost all Americans, but it has not impacted all states equally. Some states have rebounded strongly, while others continue to struggle. Why is this the case? The answer is not simple—many economic forces are at work in creating these differences, but two are of particular importance: (1) the varying responses of state and local governments to the economic downturn, and (2) the impacts of federal stimulus spending across states.

Those states that increased expenditures the most were less harmed by the Great Recession, relative to those that increased expenditures the least.

In this month's employment analysis, the Hamilton Project examines the effects of government policy in the rates of recovery among states and nationwide. Our survey of new evidence indicates that states that expanded government spending more (due in large part to support from federal stimulus during the recession) experienced smaller increases in their unemployment rates. This conclusion comes from a pair of new academic studies on the American Recovery and Reinvestment Act (ARRA) or the 2009 stimulus plan; both studies find robust evidence that government policy helped reduce the extent of the downturn and improve job growth. We also continue to explore the nation's "jobs gap," or the number of jobs that the U.S. economy needs to create in order to return to pre-recession employment levels.

There is much debate about whether and how government policies have helped to speed America's recovery from the Great Recession. One argument is that government policies helped foster a recovery by increasing spending and reducing taxes to support workers, consumers, and businesses. An alternative view, however, sees this approach as neutral at best and counterproductive at worst.

The response of federal and state governments to the Great Recession provides an opportunity to collect evidence that sheds light on the issue. Federal policies affected some states more than others, and some states changed policies more than others, providing a real-life laboratory to examine the role of government policy by comparing the outcomes of different states that were treated and acted differently. By comparing expenditures and unemployment rates among the states, we find that those states that increased expenditures the most were less harmed by the Great Recession, relative to those that increased expenditures the least. . . .

The Relationship Between State Spending and Employment

Unemployment during this period increased across the country because of the onset of the Great Recession. The increase in the nation's unemployment rate from 2007 to 2010 was 5 percentage points. However, among those states that increased expenditures the least, the average unemployment rate increased by nearly 5.2 percentage points. On the other hand, states that increased expenditures the most experienced the smallest increase in unemployment (3.9 percentage points).

One source of this relationship is straightforward: Hiring or retaining more teachers or emergency first responders means fewer people looking for work. But there are indirect effects too, as these teachers and emergency responders have money to spend, thereby increasing demand for goods and services in other areas of the economy. As a result, these increases in state spending do not just add to government jobs but add to employment across the economy.

Of course, there are numerous other factors at play in this relationship between spending and unemployment. States that were in better economic condition may have been in better fiscal shape and therefore had more flexibility to increase spending. For example, the government of North Dakota increased per capita spending by more than 31 percent, and the state experienced the smallest rise in unemployment. But North Dakota also experienced the fortuitous expansion of gas and oil production, which increased both economic activity and employment and also filled the government's coffers. In this case, a healthier economy may have also led to more

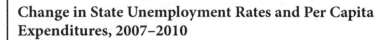

Change in State Unemployment Rates and Per Capita Expenditures, 2007–2010

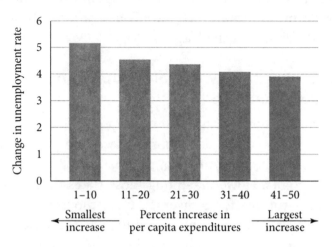

Original source: BLS and Census

spending, rather than more spending simply leading to a healthier economy. While the data are therefore suggestive, it is important [to] draw on more rigorous studies to isolate the effect of stimulative spending policies during recent years.

States that increased expenditures the most experienced the smallest increase in unemployment.

The Importance of Stimulus Spending

The Great Recession and the implementation of ARRA provide a natural laboratory to examine the effect of government spending on employment. Two new studies take advantage of quirks in funding laws that caused some states to get more money for reasons that were plausibly unrelated to their economic prospects in order to explore the impact of stimulus on states. Below is a summary of two peer-reviewed, soon-to-be published empirical studies showing the direct causal relationship between ARRA spending and economic performance.

A paper by Gabriel Chodorow-Reich, Laura Feiveson, Zachary Liscow, and William Gui Woolston examines how grants to states included in ARRA affected state government spending and local labor markets. States with higher Medicaid spending before the recession received more stimulus dollars than others according to the allocation formula. For example, the state of Utah received $103 per person as of June 2010, while the District of Columbia received $507 per person. These differences in spending translated into big differences in employment. The authors estimate that an additional $100,000 in Medicaid aid to a state results in an additional 3.8 job-years, the great majority of which are outside the government, education, and health care sectors.

Similarly, Daniel J. Wilson investigates how differences in ARRA funding to states affected employment. Wilson takes a broad approach by examining more than Medicaid funding, taking advantage of the fact that states with more highway miles or with other characteristics unrelated to economic conditions tended to receive more stimulus money. He determines that stimulus spending had a significant impact within the first year of implementation and that each $125,000 in additional spending increased employment by about one job.

Of course, these estimates of the "cost per job" overstate the actual cost because they neglect the services provided by the spending. These funds were spent on fixing or improving infrastructure, bettering the education system, and reducing hardship in families of the unemployed—costs that would have been incurred in the future anyway and services with real value. All of the evidence, taken together, therefore points to a clear finding: The ARRA stimulus program played an important role in boosting employment in the wake of the recession.

The Jobs Gap

As of June, our nation faces a "jobs gap" of 11.3 million jobs. . . .

If the economy adds about 208,000 jobs per month, which was the average monthly rate for the best year of job creation in the 2000s, then it will take until June 2020—or eight years—to close the jobs gap. Given a more optimistic rate of 321,000 jobs per month, which was the average monthly rate of the best year of job creation in the 1990s, the economy will reach pre-recession employment levels by August 2016—not for another four years. . . .

The ARRA stimulus program played an important role in boosting employment in the wake of the recession.

The Great Recession resulted in significant increases in unemployment, but it did not impact all states equally. In fact, one contributor to the disparities appears to have been the differences in state government spending. Those states that increased per capita expenditures the most experienced the smallest rises in unemployment rates, while those that increased expenditures the least experienced the largest rises in unemployment. Although state governments certainly played a role in shaping their economic situations, much of the increased state spending was financed by the American Recovery and Reinvestment Act (the federal stimulus plan), which put significant amounts of money directly into depleted state coffers.

Given the serious challenge of the long-run budget outlook, it will be necessary to take difficult steps to address the imbalance between what the federal government spends and how much it raises in revenues. But it is also important to recognize that, despite the boost from the temporary stimulus, millions of Americans remain out of work and more than 40 percent of the unemployed have not worked for six months or longer. As policy makers grapple with these dual fiscal and economic challenges, it is important to recognize that they need not be at odds. The best prescription for improving the budget deficit over the next few years is to return the economy to health. To that end, it is instructive to consider the latest evidence that active budget policies enacted today can help boost employment and speed recovery.

Stimulus Spending Is Not the Solution to Reducing Unemployment Worldwide

Raghuram Rajan

In the following viewpoint, Raghuram Rajan argues that the use of government spending to fix lagging demand caused by the recent economic recession is misguided. Rajan claims that the lack of consumer demand caused by a bust following a debt-fueled boom is different from the demand resulting from a cyclical recession. He concludes that the sustainable solution is to allow adjustments in the economy, not to engage in stimulus spending. Rajan is a professor of finance at the University of Chicago Booth School of Business and the chief economic adviser in India's finance ministry.

As you read, consider the following questions:

1. According to the author, what two fundamental beliefs are behind economic policies worldwide in recent years?

2. Rajan claims that economic recovery following a lending bust typically requires workers to do what?

3. What country does Rajan use as a cautionary tale against using government spending to address economic recession caused by a housing bust?

Two fundamental beliefs have driven economic policy around the world in recent years. The first is that the world suffers from a shortage of aggregate demand relative to supply; the second is that monetary and fiscal stimulus will close the gap.

The Problem of High Unemployment

Is it possible that the diagnosis is right, but that the remedy is wrong? That would explain why we have made little headway so far in restoring growth to pre-crisis levels. And it would also indicate that we must rethink our remedies.

High levels of involuntary unemployment throughout the advanced economics suggest that demand lags behind potential supply. While unemployment is significantly higher in sectors that were booming before the crisis, such as construction in the United States, it is more widespread, underpinning the view that greater demand is necessary to restore full employment.

Policy makers initially resorted to government spending and low interest rates to boost demand. As government debt has ballooned and policy interest rates have hit rock bottom, central banks have focused on increasingly innovative policy to boost demand. Yet growth continues to be painfully slow. Why?

The Uniqueness of Debt-Fueled Demand

What if the problem is the assumption that all demand is created equal? We know that pre-crisis demand was boosted by massive amounts of borrowing. When borrowing becomes easier, it is not the well-to-do, whose spending is not constrained by their incomes, who increase their consumption; rather, the increase comes from poorer and younger families whose needs and dreams far outpace their incomes. Their needs can be different from those of the rich.

Moreover, the goods that are easiest to buy are those that are easy to post as collateral—houses and cars, rather than perishables. And rising house prices in some regions make it easier to borrow even more to spend on other daily needs such as diapers and baby food.

It is easy to see why a general stimulus to demand, such as a cut in payroll taxes, may be ineffective in restoring the economy to full employment.

The point is that debt-fueled demand emanates from particular households in particular regions for particular goods. While it catalyzes a more generalized demand—the elderly plumber who works longer hours in the boom spends more on his stamp collection—it is not unreasonable to believe that much of debt-fueled demand is more focused. So, as lending dries up, borrowing households can no longer spend, and demand for certain goods changes disproportionately, especially in areas that boomed earlier.

Of course, the effects spread through the economy—as demand for cars falls, demand for steel also falls, and steel workers are laid off. But unemployment is most pronounced in the construction and automobile sectors, or in regions where house prices rose particularly rapidly.

The Problem with Stimulus Spending

It is easy to see why a general stimulus to demand, such as a cut in payroll taxes, may be ineffective in restoring the economy to full employment. The general stimulus goes to everyone, not just the former borrowers. And everyone's spending patterns differ—the older, wealthier household buys jewelry from Tiffany, rather than a car from General Motors. And even the former borrowers are unlikely to use their stimulus money to pay for more housing—they have soured on the dreams that housing held out.

Indeed, because the pattern of demand that is expressible has shifted with the change in access to borrowing, the pace at which the economy can grow without inflation may also fall. With too many construction workers and too few jewelers, greater demand may result in higher jewelry prices rather than more output.

Put differently, the bust that follows years of a debt-fueled boom leaves behind an economy that supplies too much of the wrong kind of good relative to the changed demand. Unlike a normal cyclical recession, in which demand falls across the board and recovery requires merely rehiring laid-off workers to resume their old jobs, economic recovery following a lending bust typically requires workers to move across industries and to new locations.

The worst thing that governments can do is to stand in the way by propping up unviable firms or by sustaining demand in unviable industries through easy credit.

There is thus a subtle but important difference between my debt-driven demand view and the neo-Keynesian [referring to the economic theories and programs ascribed to John Maynard Keynes] explanation that de-leveraging (saving by chastened borrowers) or debt overhang (the inability of debt-laden borrowers to spend) is responsible for slow post-crisis growth. Both views accept that the central source of weak aggregate demand is the disappearance of demand from former borrowers. But they differ on solutions.

The neo-Keynesian economist wants to boost demand generally. But if we believe that debt-driven demand is different, demand stimulus will at best be a palliative. Writing down former borrowers' debt may be slightly more effective in producing the old pattern of demand, but it will probably not restore it to the pre-crisis level. In any case, do we really want the former borrowers to borrow themselves into trouble again?

A Sustainable Solution

The only sustainable solution is to allow the supply side to adjust to more normal and sustainable sources of demand—to ease the way for construction workers and autoworkers to re-train for faster-growing industries. The worst thing that governments can do is to stand in the way by propping up unviable firms or by sustaining demand in unviable industries through easy credit.

Supply-side adjustments take time, and, after five years of recession, economies have made some headway. But continued misdiagnosis will have lasting effects. The advanced countries will spend decades working off high public-debt loads, while their central banks will have to unwind bloated balance sheets and back off from promises of support that markets have come to rely on.

Frighteningly, the new Japanese government is still trying to deal with the aftermath of the country's two-decade-old property bust. One can only hope that it will not indulge in more of the kind of spending that already has proven so ineffective—and that has left Japan with the highest debt burden (around 230% of GDP [gross domestic product]) in the OECD [Organisation for Economic Co-operation and Development]. Unfortunately, history provides little cause for optimism.

In the Arab World, an Economic Revolution Is Needed to Allow Job Creation

Mina Al Oraibi and Yasar Jarrar

In the following viewpoint, Mina Al Oraibi and Yasar Jarrar argue that the uprisings in the Arab world illustrate the need for an economic and political revolution that addresses the problem of youth unemployment. Al Oraibi and Jarrar claim that a paradigm shift in thinking is needed to allow the private sector to create growth, moving power away from the public sector and creating a development paradox. Al Oraibi is assistant editor in chief for Asharq Al-Awsat, an Arabic international newspaper headquartered in London. Jarrar is partner at Bain & Company in the United Arab Emirates.

As you read, consider the following questions:

1. Many people point to what issue as the key driver of the uprisings in the Arab world, according to the viewpoint?

2. Chronic unemployment in Tunisia a year after the revolution there was what percentage, according to the authors?

Mina Al Oraibi and Yasar Jarrar, "A Paradigm Shift in Government—From Creating Jobs to Enabling Job Creation," in *Addressing the 100 Million Youth Challenge: Perspectives on Youth Employment in the Arab World in 2012*, World Economic Forum, 2012, pp. 30–32. Copyright © 2012 by World Economic Forum. All rights reserved. Reproduced by permission.

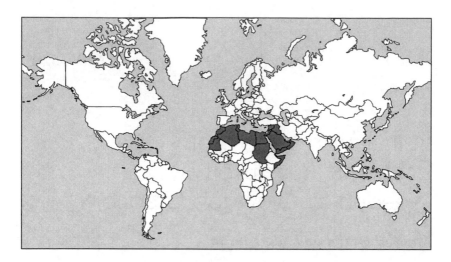

3. According to the authors, the reforms they suggest entail what paradox?

Have we witnessed an Arab Spring, or were the events of the past two years [2010–2012] a set of bread riots that were consequently glossed over by an overenthusiastic media? The answer lies somewhere along that spectrum, and differs from one person to another and from one country to the other.

The Tipping Point

Whatever the political outcomes of the historic events of 2011 will be, it must not be forgotten that these did not start as ideological revolutions, despite some emerging governments being ideologically inclined. These were also not revolutions orchestrated by charismatic leaders with a set agenda or a unified vision. These were uprisings against stolen futures—a loss of hope for a better tomorrow. Young and old people alike reached a tipping point; one that was built on broken government promises and on institutionalized and widespread corruption on various levels and across sectors.

In recent decades, rising living standards and literacy rates, as well as the increased availability of higher education, have resulted in an improved human development index in Arab countries. At the same time, technology and media were revolutionized, and the Arab citizen was empowered with information access—and the ability to transmit information, thanks to social media across and beyond borders. These trends were not coupled with sustainable economic development, nor political reform and inclusion. The result was a natural tension between rising aspirations, needs and knowledge, and a lack of economic opportunities and political participation.

For those of us from the Arab world who grew up living this tension, the main surprise was how long it took for the tipping point to be reached. It was never a matter of whether it would actually happen, rather of how and when the untenable status quo would give way. The same question still applies to some Arab countries where uprisings have not spread—unless radical and genuine reforms are delivered, fast.

Young and old people alike reached a tipping point.

We got our answer in 2011. It took the mix of a growing youth bulge, unprecedented levels of corruption and "elite" control of national wealth, a technology revolution that rendered parts of the state control vulnerable and not in control, and a global financial crisis. The combination of demographics, bad governance, development of ICTs [information and communication technologies] and diversification of media, underpinned by overwhelmingly difficult living conditions and lack of public finances to prop up the fragile system, led to an unprecedented shake up, if not collapse, of the status quo.

This overwhelming mix of frustration and a sense of stolen futures was ignited by a spark from a vegetable seller in Tunisia who could not take one more blow from the state.

161

The story of Mohamed Bouazizi has gained legendary status because it exemplified the state of mind—and heart—of so many across the Arab world.[1]

The Economic and Political Challenges

Now, and after the initial euphoria of people taking to the streets and perceiving an immediate impact, it is evident that what happened was only the beginning of a decade of changes that will sweep through the whole Arab world. The future is not clear, and no one can claim to predict where it is heading, but what is certain is that it will never look the same again, nor will fear alone be a tool to govern.

The generation demanding the change today is different from the generations that preceded them. One of these differences is that access to technology enabled them to compare themselves to others on a daily basis—their living standards, their future hopes and aspirations and their governments and governors. The comparison was not favourable for many. Today, young people's expectations are high and will continue to increase, and it appears that they will not be told what to think, or who to thank.

In trying to understand the reasons behind these revolutions, many point to the issue of high unemployment as the key driver, identifying it as a primary indicator of the loss of hope and frustration driving young people to revolt. Yet this dynamic cannot be taken out of context.

All too often, the political challenges of the region are disassociated from the economic ones. While officials are comfortable discussing economic pitfalls, they veer away from the political reasons behind them (or at least compounding them). [As Jordanian former prime minister Awn Shawkat Al-

---

1. In an act of desperation on December 17, 2010, 26-year-old Mohamed Bouazizi set himself on fire to protest the government and economic conditions in Tunisia that fueled uprisings in that country and across the Middle East.

Khasawneh said,] "One cannot be a reformist in his economics and reactionary in his politics."

The Problem of Youth Exclusion

The reactions to the events of 2011 among Arab countries varied in speed and scale. Some rushed to increase, or even double, the wages of civil servants; others chose political gestures as far and wide as introducing major amendments to their constitutions. Yet the flurry of activity was often to placate in the short term, with longer-term demands, especially of the youth, either still being worked out or ignored altogether. So far, we saw a plethora of Band-Aids, but the actual wounds are still open, painful and getting worse. What is more worrying is these Band-Aids and knee-jerk social hand outs are very expensive, often leading to either increasing state deficit or ever-rising break-even oil prices in oil-producing countries. For those nations opting for more structured reforms, generous funding will be required to turn things around and restart nation building on the inefficient "institutional rubble" that is today's public sector.

So where would a nation start? In addition to ineffective and overinflated government institutions, there is no shortage of challenges impairing Arab economies, such as ineffective subsidies, the overuse of regulations, a mismatch between education and the workplace, youth unemployment, weak entrepreneurial base, mushrooming deficits and a deficit of meritocracy. And yet these are not unknown ailments and have been discussed in the past many times over.

A key manifestation of the above challenges is the current state of youth exclusion in the region. Youth unemployment in the Middle East is the highest in the world—estimated to be at 30%. These developmental challenges are a failure of public policy thinking and execution (i.e., a failure of both governance structures and government performance). They do not arise from a lack of information about what needs to be done. The core policy solutions to youth unemployment have been long known and widely discussed for some time now. They focus on a comprehensive group of policy reforms, including reforming education to promote opportunities and incentives to develop a range of market-applicable and adaptive skills; ending the ineffective reliance on inflated public sector employment by rationalizing government hiring; reforming wage and non-wage practices and policies; improving labour market regulations by introducing more flexibility into hiring and firing decisions; easing business start-up regulations; improving access to credit; and introducing effective social protection schemes, such as like unemployment insurance.

Yet the will and ability to actually tackle the issues at stake remained missing. Officials in the region knew about the challenges, discussed them in hundreds of conferences and openly talked about the 100 million jobs needed by 2020. Across the whole of the Arab world, there were plenty of words but few deeds.

Youth unemployment in the Middle East is the highest in the world—estimated to be at 30%.

The Need for an Economic Revolution

Today we face a crisis of leadership. Can we expect policies for a better future to be designed and delivered by the same government institutions that have been neglected for decades and are quite often inefficient and ineffective? Can we expect the current civil service, which has been mostly a social employer in many cases in the Arab world, to suddenly handle complex public policy needs effectively and create public value? More importantly, can we expect the top-down approach to be the way forward in tackling these challenges? Many still believe that "government knows best," and both leaders and the populace can fall into the trap of seeing it as the only feasible plan.

The inconvenient truth is that it will take a decade, if not decades, to rebuild these state institutions, to develop the civil service capabilities and to regain public trust. The road ahead is long and hard. There are no silver bullets, and whatever frustrations the youth had which led to the uprising will only grow over the coming years when they see that, despite some political reforms, what we really need is an economic revolution.

Unemployed people voting in open elections will not be the route to a better tomorrow, despite the expected, and welcome, cheers from democracy enthusiasts—it is simply not enough. In Tunisia, almost a year and a half after the ousting of Zine El Abidine Ben Ali, the revolution has so far brought little tangible improvement in living standards. Chronic unemployment has risen since the revolution, standing a year later at 19%, and the country recently saw various crowds of young men attacking government buildings to protest what they said was a slow response by the authorities to their immediate needs. In attempting to deal with the crisis, the government has pledged 25,000 civil service jobs this year. This is not the solution; it is simply a repeat of past mistakes.

We need an economic revolution that is beyond rhetoric, ideologies and blaming others for our past failures. This is needed at a time when even the most advanced economies are struggling to create jobs for their own people. According to the International Labour Organization, 12.7% of youth around the world were unemployed in 2011. In the United Kingdom [UK], unemployment among those under 25 years of age reached 20.3% last year, while Brazil has similar levels.

This economic revolution needs to be underlined by a shift in mind-sets towards real innovations in governance and economic growth. Governments cannot go on running "business as usual," subsidizing welfare, controlling the media and simply creating more civil service jobs. International organizations coming to the region with "one-size-fits-all" models will not be successful either. Solutions need to be unique and tailored to each country. Many will not forget how in 2007–2008 the World Bank praised Tunisia as an exemplar Arab country in economic reform and the Egyptian government as "top global reformer" in its Doing Business report of 2010.

A Paradigm Shift in Thinking

What is needed now is a paradigm shift in thinking about job creation. Governments should stop speaking of their plans for job creation and should start implementing policies for enabling job creation. This is not a simple academic argument or a semantic one. Governments and citizens have to accept that governments cannot do it by themselves anymore. What governments should do is to develop policies that create the enabling environment for the private sector and civil society to ensure that jobs are created and transparent decisions are taken and upheld.

What is needed now is a paradigm shift in thinking about job creation.

The solution rests in the ability to balance government measures and to unleash enablers in society—and particularly the private sector—to catalyse the dynamism and innovation of the youth. Public value will have to be created via a deliberate and well-structured collaboration among the public sector, private sector and civil society. While this is a major paradigm shift in the Arab world, it is by no means a novel idea. The world over, governments are reinventing themselves along those lines, including the current UK's Big Society, and the Open Government initiative being adopted by various countries around the world. Everyone is searching for the "new normal" in governance.

Governments in the Arab world should focus less on expanding the civil service and creating public sector jobs and more on providing the space for others to participate in job creation; they should expedite freeing up their markets and improving competition. This clearly implies breaking up decades of monopoly and elite control of the economic sectors. This will not be easy and will generate resistance from powerful, vested-interest stakeholders. Steps should be taken to reduce red tape and simplify the process for starting a business and to eliminate the institutionalized corruption that is embedded in the process. Dubai [a city in the United Arab Emirates] provides a clear example from within the region—setting up a business there is at times easier than it is in the United States. And while some point to the fiscal troubles of Dubai as an excuse to write off some of its achievements, it would be short-sighted to dismiss the lessons learned in Dubai and the success made possible there by limiting bureaucracy and government modernization. Dubai remains the number one destination Arab youth site as their first choice to live and work.

Governments in the Arab world should focus less on expanding the civil service and creating public sector jobs and more on providing the space for others to participate in job creation.

The Need for Social Change

In parallel, governments also need to remove limitations on freedom of expression, which in large part has begun with the rise of the Internet and social media, and yet they must accept the change and adapt to it, not continue to fight and censor it—that is an expensive and losing battle. Most importantly, governments need to "walk the talk" when it comes to fighting corruption. The easiest way to demonstrate how sincere these attempts are is to adopt policies regarding open government data, and share transparent information on performance and public finances. Open government data enables the citizens and media to scrutinize and weed out improper financial and regulatory behaviour; it empowers business with hard-to-find data for growth and development; and enables new start-ups in innovative public and private services. The state has long been the biggest generator, collector and user of data in most countries. As the information revolution reshapes the business landscape, governments have responded by returning data to the hands of the people who paid for it.

Countries in the region should also start thinking outside their own geographic boxes. There is a compelling imperative to seriously start looking at some form of genuine economic collaboration. Many of the region's countries are too small (by economic size, population, geography, global political weight, or all these combined) to tackle the complex policy issues facing them. This holds true for transnational issues such as water security and food security, as well as more local issues of job creation. What happens in Yemen is a core concern for Jordan's future, and Dubai's trade is dependent on a healthy and stable Iraq.

Another major shift is needed in how governments perceive and treat civil society organizations. Civil society must be allowed and encouraged to develop and flourish. No society can simply be split between governments and business—there is a need for the essential third sphere of civil society organizations to foster development. In many countries, NGOs [nongovernmental organizations] have been the first responders to crises, and a major driver in youth education and employment. Governments in the Arab world should curb their regulations of civil societies and NGOs and embrace them as major players in creating jobs and public value. This is an area that has major potential, especially in a region where the Islamic tradition of *Waqf* is well developed. Foundations can flourish, and philanthropy can be a major development driver, especially on social and economic local issues. It is such organizations that have been hailed the "great American secret" behind powerful development in the United States' education and knowledge society.

The Region's Development Paradox

All of these elements could combine to create a dynamic of change and an environment conducive to job creation—or, more importantly, opportunity creation. However, the crucial factor is the change in mind-sets to allow the success of any or all of the above policy suggestions to unleash the talent of young entrepreneurs, business entrepreneurs and social entrepreneurs, and to generate entrepreneurship in the public sector and innovations in creating public value.

James Caan, the leading British-Pakistani serial entrepreneur and media leader has noted, "being an entrepreneur means striving to control your destiny." It is the battle over this control—from the family structure to the political systems in place—that inevitably will determine the talent that is born and fostered in the region.

Civil society must be allowed and encouraged to develop and flourish.

When we speak of talent and opportunity, this cannot simply mean the ability to rise in certain spheres and not in others—that a company can succeed, as long as it does not impose on the business interests of the ruling elite, or a young man or woman can dream of rising to the top ranks of a multinational organization but never the top ranks of government. Yes, the silver bullet is meritocracy.

These reforms will mean the curtailing of powers and privileges of the very people who need to lead and implement the changes. This is the region's development paradox: Reforms have to be undertaken by the same people who stand to

169

lose, in the short term, from their implementation. However, everyone realizes that this is not merely a moral imperative, but a realistic one for survival.

South Africa's Unemployment Puzzle

Abebe Aemro Selassie

In the following viewpoint, Abebe Aemro Selassie argues that addressing high unemployment is a top priority for South Africa. Selassie contends that although the recession in South Africa was mild, the job losses were severe, partly a result of a lack of wage moderation. Selassie claims that the solutions to unemployment are higher growth, targeted interventions to decrease youth unemployment, and increased competition. Selassie is an assistant director in the International Monetary Fund's European Department and is currently mission chief for Portugal.

As you read, consider the following questions:

1. According to Selassie, what percentage of South African youth are unemployed?

2. What happened to South African wages in 2009, according to the author?

3. Selassie proposes that economic growth double from what current rate?

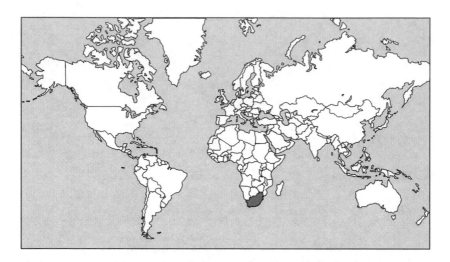

*A*mong the havoc wrought by the global financial crisis, un-employment ranks at the top. This discussion often focuses on the situation in advanced countries. Unemployment in the United States, for example, continues to hover around 9 percent.

Take that and double it. Then you can begin—yes, just begin—to get a sense of the magnitude of the problem in South Africa. *Unemployment in South Africa now stands at some 24 percent. Youth unemployment is phenomenally higher still at some 50 percent.*

Unemployment in South Africa was already very high before the crisis due to a number of structural factors—such as mismatches between the kinds of jobs available and workers' skills, or large distances between population centers and where businesses are located.

But, the enormous job losses during 2008–09 made the already dire situation much worse. South Africa did not have a financial crisis and its recession was, relatively speaking, mild. Still, the country lost proportionately as many formal sector jobs (1 million) as those countries at the center of the global financial crisis.

Like the government, we see reducing unemployment as the foremost economic challenge facing the country. Trying to understand why recent labor market outcomes have been so bad and, more important still, what it will take to reverse the increase in unemployment is thus an ongoing focus of our work.

Unemployment in South Africa now stands at some 24 percent.

Pieces to the Puzzle

One interesting finding is that, despite high unemployment, South Africa's labor markets are relatively dynamic. *During the growth upswing of the mid-2000s, the country was very good at creating jobs; but when the economy hits a rough patch, job losses also tend to be very high.* For each 1 percentage point increase in growth, employment growth tends to increase by more than 1 percentage point. Unfortunately, the same is true when growth declines.

This goes some way towards explaining the relatively large magnitude of job shedding during the recent recession. But it also implies that wages do not respond much to changes in the demand for labor. When there is an adverse shock to demand, it is the level of employment rather than wages that adjust. Of course, in most countries, wages are generally 'sticky' downwards and do not decline in nominal terms. But seldom does one also see large economy-wide increases in real wages— wages rising faster than inflation—during a recession. Yet, that is exactly what happened in South Africa in 2009.

Last December I had the opportunity to meet with some members of South Africa's parliament. We exchanged views on the impact of the global financial crisis on the country. When I laid out the ideas above, one of the members asked if I thought that the country's employment protection laws were the cause. As I noted then, this is not my view. *Indeed, I firmly believe that the country's labor legislation provides important and necessary—and hard won—protection for workers. Rather, what would be worthwhile is a close look at the wage bargaining framework to ensure that most of the adjustment in the labor market does not continue to fall mainly on the number of jobs.* Wage moderation during downturns would not seem that unreasonable a trade-off.

Likely Solutions

Beyond a more flexible wage bargaining framework, here's my take on what is required to make significant inroads into high unemployment in South Africa.

Higher Growth. The government's recent budget document noted that annual growth of the order of 6–7 percent will be needed to meet the target of creating 5 million jobs by 2020. The current fairly supportive monetary and fiscal policies will help in the near term. But it is unclear where the impetus for the higher growth will come from once macroeconomic policies turn less supportive, with a view to rebuilding the policy buffers run down over the last couple of years. Ideally, growth should be private investment and export led. Looking for ways to promote private investment thus needs to be firmly on the reform agenda in the coming months.

Making Growth More Labor Intensive. Another approach that should help is targeted interventions to address unemployment in particularly problematic areas—such as youth unemployment. This is, in part, because current wage-setting mechanisms do not allow differences in wages that would fully reflect productivity differences between young and old workers. A wage subsidy scheme along the lines recently announced by the government should serve to make it cheaper

South African Government Response to Unemployment

To address unemployment, the authorities are focused on orienting economic policy to raise potential growth and increase its labor intensity. To this end, the government has emphasized that its infrastructure construction program, intended to relieve bottlenecks in electricity and transport, would raise potential growth over the medium term and foster more job creation. Electricity remains a key constraint on economic activity, and lower transport costs, would not only reduce the cost of business, but make it easier for workers to commute to jobs, helping to overcome the legacy of spatial separation. The authorities have also noted that elements of this infrastructure program have been designed to be labor intensive, helping to facilitate faster job growth in the short run.

The government is also contemplating more direct interventions in the labor market, such as a wage subsidy aimed at younger workers. Current labor market institutions do not allow for the productivity gap between young and older workers to be reflected fully in wage differentials and so unemployment among young labor force entrants is phenomenally high at some 50 percent. The wage subsidy, if introduced, would make it cheaper for firms to employ young unskilled workers, helping to build skills and enhance the productivity of these workers over their careers. The authorities however noted that there is no single measure available to address unemployment, and only a combination of carefully designed initiatives as well as faster growth are likely to make significant inroads in unemployment.

Staff Representatives for the 2010 Consultation with South Africa,
"Staff Report for the 2010 Article IV Consultation,"
International Monetary Fund, September 2010.

for firms to employ young workers. Provided the subsidy is carefully designed, it should avoid the displacement of existing workers and also minimize substitution away from older workers.

Ideally, growth should be private investment and export led.

More Competitive Product Markets. One of the other problematic features of the South Africa economy is the relatively high cost structure of many of its markets for goods and services. By contributing to higher input costs, this inhibits the external competitiveness of manufacturing and other tradable sectors. Enhancing domestic competition should lower costs for companies but importantly also for consumers.

The big blemish on South Africa's otherwise strong economic performance since the mid-1990s is stubbornly high unemployment. Of course this is an important exception, especially as it has exacerbated income inequality. Doubling growth—from the current 3$^1/_2$ percent—is the first order of business. And this in turn requires changing the incentives facing firms and employees.

The United States Should Adopt German Work Hours to Lower Unemployment

Dean Baker

In the following viewpoint, Dean Baker argues that the problem of unemployment in the United States could be remedied immediately by shortening the workweek. Baker claims that the United States should emulate European countries that have shorter workweeks, thus requiring more workers for the same amount of work. In addition, he claims that Germany weathered the recession not by laying off workers, but by shortening work hours, offering this as a temporary solution at minimum. Baker is codirector of the Center for Economic and Policy Research and author of several books, including The End of Loser Liberalism: Making Markets Progressive.

As you read, consider the following questions:

1. According to the author, the problem facing wealthy countries is not that they are poor, but what?

2. The average worker in Germany and the Netherlands works how much less than the average American worker, according to Baker?

3. Baker claims that if the United States shortened work-weeks, lost wages would ideally be made up how?

Nobel laureate Paul Krugman and Richard Layard, a distinguished British economist, took the lead last week [June 27, 2012] in drafting a sign-on "A Manifesto for Economic Sense", condemning the turn toward austerity in many countries. This manifesto seems destined to garner tens or even hundreds of thousands of signatures, including mine.

The Lesson of the Great Depression

While the basic logic of the manifesto is solid, there is an important aspect to the argument that is overlooked. We can deal with unemployment every bit as effectively by having people work fewer hours, as we can by increasing demand.

The most important point to realize is that the problem facing wealthy countries at the moment is not that we are poor, as the stern proponents of austerity insist. The problem is that we are wealthy. We have tens of millions of people unemployed precisely because we can meet current demand without needing their labor.

This was the incredible absurdity of the misery that we and other countries endured during the Great Depression, and which [economist John Maynard] Keynes sought to explain in *The General Theory* [*of Employment, Interest and Money*]. The world did not suddenly turn poor in 1929, following the collapse of the stock market. Our workers had the ability to produce just as many goods and services the day after the collapse as the day before; the problem was that after the crash, there was a lack of demand for these goods and services.

We can deal with unemployment every bit as effectively by having people work fewer hours, as we can by increasing demand.

The result of this lack of demand was a decade of double-digit unemployment in the United States. The spending programs of the New Deal helped to alleviate the impact of the downturn, but because of the deficit hawks of that era, [President Franklin D.] Roosevelt never could spend enough to bring the economy back to full employment—at least until the Second World War made deficits irrelevant.

Government Policy to Address Unemployment

This is the same story we face today. The US and European economies were close to full employment in 2007 due to demand created by housing bubbles in the United States and across much of Europe. These bubbles then burst, substantially reducing demand. As Krugman and Layard point out in their statement, one remedy for this loss of demand is for government to fill the gap. If the private sector is not prepared to spend enough to bring the economy to full employment, then the government can engage in deficit spending to make up the shortfall.

But there is another dimension to this issue. It's great for the government to generate demand insofar as it can productively employ people. This means either providing immediate services, like health care and education, or in investing in areas that will provide future dividends, such as modernizing the infrastructure or retrofitting buildings to increase their energy efficiency.

However, it can also employ people by encouraging employers to divide work among more workers. There is nothing natural about the length of the average workweek or work year and there are, in fact, large variations across countries. The average worker in Germany and the Netherlands puts in 20% fewer hours in a year than the average worker in the United States. This means that if the US adopted Germany's work patterns tomorrow, it would *immediately* eliminate unemployment.

The Benefits of a Shorter Workweek

Of course, it is unrealistic to imagine such large changes occurring overnight, but governments can certainly attempt to encourage employers to shorten workweeks and increase vacation and other paid time off. In fact, this is the real secret of Germany's post-crisis recovery. Germany's growth has been no better than growth in the United States since the start of the downturn, yet its unemployment rate has fallen by 2.0 percentage points—while unemployment in the United States has risen by almost 4.0 percentage points. The difference is that Germany encourages firms to reduce work hours rather than lay off workers.

If the US adopted Germany's work patterns tomorrow, it would immediately *eliminate unemployment.*

Since workers in the United States put in the most hours, the US has the greatest potential gains from shortening work years. But all countries could try to go this path. In the short term, this route keeps people employed and allows them more

Hours Worked in Europe and America

Although most Western industrialized nations once lagged behind U.S. developments, in recent years most forged ahead while the United States fell back. In 2000, 76 percent of American workers put in forty or more hours a week—an increase from 73 percent in 1983. In England only about 50 percent worked forty or more hours a week, and in France the share of the employed working that many hours decreased from 36 percent to 22 percent between 1983 and 2000. The reduction in the workweek was even more pronounced in Germany: Only 43 percent of the workforce worked forty or more hours in 2000, down sharply from 85 percent in 1983.

In much of Europe four to six weeks of annual vacation is also now mandated by law for all workers (including newly hired workers). In the United States most workers don't receive four weeks of vacation until they've reached twenty years of service. Different methods of data collection make precise comparisons difficult. However, taking hours worked per week together with vacation time, workers in France and Germany reduced work enormously, compared to their American counterparts—by 260 hours per year between 1979 and 2000, the equivalent of cutting six and a half forty-hour weeks out of the work year!

Gar Alperovitz, America Beyond Capitalism: Reclaiming Our Wealth, Our Liberty, and Our Democracy. *Takoma Park, MD: Democracy Collaborative Press, 2011, p. 198.*

time to enjoy with their family and friends. Ideally, most of the lost wages will be made up by subsidies from the government. (Remember, the problem is too little demand, not too much. We can afford this.)

In the longer term, workers may find that they prefer more leisure and may be willing to sacrifice some income to have a shorter workweek, paid vacation or family leave, or other paid time off. If that ended up being the case, it would be a lasting benefit from using short-time working as a route for dealing with the downturn.

But even if there are no long-run changes in work patterns, shorter work hours should be on everyone's list as a mechanism to combat unemployment. It is a proven success story with real benefits for workers and the economy.

Europeans Should Migrate to Latin America to Combat Unemployment

Gillian Tett

In the following viewpoint, Gillian Tett argues that a recent suggestion that Europeans migrate to Latin America for work makes a lot of sense. Tett claims that countries such as Brazil are experiencing a shortage of qualified workers that could be filled by Europeans from countries with high unemployment. Tett contends that although migration patterns typically are from the developing world to the developed world, there is good reason to think the opposite pattern can also help balance the global economy. Tett is markets and finance columnist and assistant editor at the Financial Times, *a London-based business news and information newspaper.*

As you read, consider the following questions:

1. According to Tett, Brazil has a net need for how many engineers a year?

2. Tett refers to a report finding that how many Mexicans had immigrated to the United States over the past four decades?

Gillian Tett, "Is It Time for Europeans to Migrate?," *FT Magazine* (UK), June 15, 2012. Reproduced by permission.

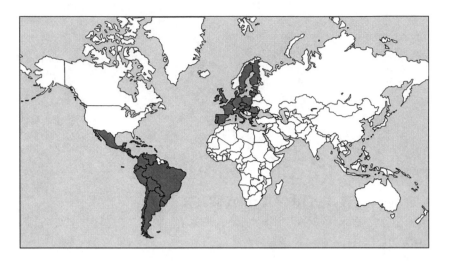

3. It has been reported, according to the author, that how many Portuguese hold work permits for Brazil?

If you say the word "migrant worker" in Washington these days, it usually evokes images of Mexican farm labourers. But last week [June 11, 2012] in Boston, at a meeting of financial leaders, the concept reared its head in a surprisingly different way: It was linked to the euro zone.

A Need for Workers

The context was a lunchtime debate about the future of global finance, at which Paulo de Sousa Oliveira, the head of Brasil Investimentos and Negócios, gave a speech selling Brazil as a financial hub. With passion, Oliveira explained why it was important for financial centres such as Boston, London and São Paulo to co-operate, and cited endless statistics showing how vibrant the Brazilian economy is these days, relative to the West.

Then, as the conversation inevitably turned to the latest euro zone horrors, Oliveira made a plea. "There is such high unemployment in Spain and Portugal, they should send their people over here [to Brazil] to get work—they can work and then send money back home [to Europe] and then go home themselves after 10 years!" he earnestly explained. After all, he added by way of example, Brazil currently needs about 60,000 engineers a year—but only 40,000 are graduating inside Brazil. So why not get those European engineers, or other young graduates, to travel as migrant workers? "We have a need for 20,000 more engineers! We have a need for migrants!" he explained. Why not use Latin America as a source of remittances for euro zone families starved of cash?

It is a telling little indication of how the world is being subtly turned on its head, amid the rolling crises. During the past five decades, if anybody has been packing their bags to travel overseas to send remittances home, it has typically been the Brazilians, or other "emerging markets" peoples, not the developed Europeans. In recent years, Spain and Portugal have been pulling in vast quantities of migrant workers, both skilled and unskilled, as Poles and other Eastern European workers have flooded to places such as the UK [United Kingdom] and Ireland. America has sucked even larger numbers of migrants, not just from Brazil but from other parts of South America. A couple of months ago, for example, the Pew Hispanic Center (PHC) in America released a fascinating report which calculated that 12 million immigrants have moved from Mexico to the US in the past four decades alone, to seek jobs and cash. "The US today has more immigrants from Mexico alone—12.0 million—than any other country in the world has from all countries of the world," the PHC report observed, noting that in absolute terms "no country has ever seen as many of its people immigrate to this country as Mexico has in the past four decades."

A Change in Immigration Flows

Yet these days the most fascinating detail of the PHC report, which echoes that Boston lunch, is that a change is afoot. Last year "the net migration flow from Mexico to the United States has stopped and may have reversed," it says, for the first time since records began.

Part of the explanation is "the weakened US job and housing construction markets, heightened border enforcement, a rise in deportations," along with "the growing dangers associated with illegal border crossings and the long-term decline in Mexico's birth rates". But another issue is the improved "broader economic conditions in Mexico". Life south of the border, in other words, is no longer quite as grim as it was before, or not relative to the risks of moving to the US.

Migration has been a powerful force for growth in human history. Fluid flows may yet be a means for a profoundly unbalanced global economy to rebalance itself.

Sadly, there is surprisingly little comparable data for other immigration flows. As Ian Goldin, an Oxford academic, has long lamented, the world lacks any centralised system to track migration flows in a timely way, let alone devise policies. Thus we do not really know how many young Portuguese or Spanish are seeking jobs in Latin America now. (Although Reuters reports that around 328,000 Portuguese hold work permits for Brazil, 50,000 more than last year, it is unclear whether these have been exercised.) Nor is it clear how many Poles are returning to their homeland from the UK or Ireland, as austerity bites there; or how many young Irish may now be seeking their fortunes overseas (yet again). While I have recently heard plenty of anecdotes at American dinner parties and conferences about how young American graduates are becoming so disillusioned with their jobs markets that they are moving "temporarily" to Brazil or India, tracking data on that American flux—if it exists—is hard.

But I hope that plenty of ambitious young Europeans do take up Oliveira's suggestion to pack their bags, at least for a while. A century ago, entrepreneurial Europeans headed to the "colonies". Retracing those steps, as those ex-colonies swell in might, is not so odd. Migration has been a powerful force for growth in human history. Fluid flows may yet be a means for a profoundly unbalanced global economy to rebalance itself. It would be nice, at least, to dream of that—particularly in Boston, a city built by Irish immigrants fleeing earlier waves of economic pain.

Periodical and Internet Sources Bibliography

The following articles have been selected to supplement the diverse views presented in this chapter.

Economist	"Rethinking the Welfare State: Asia's Next Revolution," September 8, 2012.
Peter Frase and Bhaskar Sunkara	"The Welfare State of America: A Manifesto on Building Social Democracy in the Age of Austerity," *In These Times*, November 2012.
Robin Harding	"Central Bankers Give Voice to a Revolution," *Financial Times* (UK), December 14, 2012.
Japan Times	"Supporting the Unemployed," November 22, 2011.
Miles Johnson	"Spanish Youth Urged to Seek Work Abroad," *Financial Times* (UK), May 2, 2012.
Michael Lind	"The Age of Turboparalysis: Why We Haven't Had a Revolution," *Spectator* (UK), December 15, 2012.
Nelipher Moyo and Olumide Taiwo	"The Crisis in Tunisia: Africa's Youth Unemployment Time-Bomb," Brookings Institution, January 26, 2011. www.brookings.edu.
Kenneth Rapoza	"Brazil Discovers How to Increase Employment with Near-Zero Economic Growth," *Forbes*, June 21, 2012.
Thero Setiloane	"Beyond Advocacy—Business Needs to Get Its Head in the Game," McKinsey & Company, April 2012. http://voices.mckinseyonsociety.com.
Jordan Weissmann	"53% of Recent College Grads Are Jobless or Underemployed—How?," *Atlantic*, April 23, 2012.

For Further Discussion

Chapter 1

1. Drawing on the viewpoints of this chapter, do you think unemployment is always a serious problem? Why or why not?

Chapter 2

1. Don Peck argues that men in the United States suffer disproportionately from unemployment, whereas Guadalupe Cruz Jaime argues that women in Mexico suffer disproportionately from unemployment. Can you think of any factor that would explain this difference with respect to gender and unemployment in the two countries? Explain.

2. Tom Orlik discusses the problem migrant workers in China face in being able to collect unemployment benefits, and Suzy Freeman-Greene argues that Australia's unemployed do not receive enough unemployment benefits. Does society have a duty to provide sufficient compensation for those who are unemployed? Give one reason in favor of this view and one reason against it.

Chapter 3

1. Assessing the various viewpoints in this chapter, name four of the different causes of unemployment identified. Utilizing an example of two countries of your choosing, make an argument explaining why the cause of unemployment in one country might be different than the cause of unemployment in another country.

Chapter 4

1. Michael Greenstone and Adam Looney advocate stimulus spending as a solution to unemployment, whereas Raghuram Rajan claims that such spending will not work in the wake of the Great Recession. Does the evidence provided by Greenstone and Looney refute Rajan's argument? Why or why not?

2. Raise one objection to Dean Baker's proposal to lower unemployment in the United States by adopting shorter workweeks. Why might this not work? Explain.

Organizations to Contact

The editors have compiled the following list of organizations concerned with the issues debated in this book. The descriptions are derived from materials provided by the organizations. All have publications or information available for interested readers. The list was compiled on the date of publication of the present volume; the information provided here may change. Be aware that many organizations take several weeks or longer to respond to inquiries, so allow as much time as possible.

Adam Smith Institute

23 Great Smith Street, London SW1P 3BL
   United Kingdom
(44) 20 7222 4995
e-mail: info@adamsmith.org
website: www.adamsmith.org

The Adam Smith Institute is a libertarian think tank in the United Kingdom. Through its research, education programs, and media appearances, it promotes free markets, limited government, and an open society. The Adam Smith Institute publishes articles and reports, such as "Why Migration Watch Is Wrong About Immigration and Unemployment."

American Enterprise Institute for Public Policy Research (AEI)

1150 Seventeenth Street NW, Washington, DC 20036
(202) 862-5800 • fax: (202) 862-7177
e-mail: info@aei.org
website: www.aei.org

The American Enterprise Institute for Public Policy Research (AEI) is a private, nonpartisan, not-for-profit institution dedicated to research and education on issues of government, politics, economics, and social welfare. AEI sponsors research and publishes materials toward the end of defending the principles, and improving the institutions, of American freedom and democratic capitalism. Among AEI's publications is the online magazine the *American*.

Brookings Institution

1775 Massachusetts Avenue NW, Washington, DC   20036
(202) 797-6000
e-mail: communications@brookings.edu
website: www.brookings.edu

The Brookings Institution is a nonprofit public policy organization that conducts independent research. The Brookings Institution uses its research to provide recommendations that advance the goals of strengthening American democracy, fostering social welfare and security, and securing a cooperative international system. The Brookings Institution publishes a variety of books, journals, and reports, including "The Importance of Unemployment Insurance for American Families and the Economy."

Center for American Progress (CAP)

1333 H Street NW, 10th Floor, Washington, DC   20005
(202) 682-1611 • fax: (202) 682-1867
website: www.americanprogress.org

The Center for American Progress (CAP) is a nonprofit, nonpartisan organization dedicated to improving the lives of Americans through progressive ideas and action. CAP dialogues with leaders, thinkers, and citizens to explore the vital issues facing America and the world. CAP publishes numerous research papers, which are available at its website, including "The High Cost of Youth Unemployment."

Centre for Economic Policy Research (CEPR)

77 Bastwick Street, London   EC1V 3PZ
   United Kingdom
(44) 20 7183 8801 • fax: (44) 20 7183 8820

e-mail: cepr@cepr.org
website: www.cepr.org

The Centre for Economic Policy Research (CEPR) is the leading European research network in economics. CEPR gathers information through a network of academic researches and disseminates the results to the private sector and policy community. CEPR produces a wide range of reports, books, and conference volumes each year, including "Financial Shocks, Unemployment, and Public Policy."

Economic Policy Institute (EPI)

1333 H Street NW, Suite 300, East Tower
Washington, DC   20005-4707
(202) 775-8810 • fax: (202) 775-0819
e-mail: epi@epi.org
website: www.epi.org

The Economic Policy Institute (EPI) is a nonprofit think tank that seeks to broaden the discussion about economic policy to include the interests of low- and middle-income workers. EPI briefs policy makers at all levels of government; provides technical support to national, state, and local activists and community organizations; testifies before national, state, and local legislatures; and provides information and background to the print and electronic media. EPI publishes books, studies, issue briefs, popular education materials, and other publications, among which is the biennially published "State of Working America."

Institute for America's Future (IAF)

1825 K Street NW, Suite 400, Washington, DC   20006
(202) 955-5665 • fax: (202) 955-5606
website: institute.ourfuture.org

The Institute for America's Future (IAF) works to equip Americans with the tools and information needed to drive issues into the national debate, challenge failed conservative policies, and build support for the progressive vision of a government that is on the side of working people. Drawing on a network of scholars, activists, and leaders across the country, IAF develops policy ideas, educational materials, and outreach programs. Publications of IAF include "The Unemployment Crisis That Jobs Legislation Must Address."

International Monetary Fund (IMF)

700 Nineteenth Street NW, Washington, DC   20431
(202) 623-7000 • fax: (202) 623-4661
e-mail: publicaffairs@imf.org
website: www.imf.org

The International Monetary Fund (IMF) is an organization of 186 countries working to foster global monetary cooperation, secure financial stability, facilitate international trade, promote high employment and sustainable economic growth, and reduce poverty around the world. The IMF monitors the world's economies, lends to members in economic difficulty, and provides technical assistance. The IMF publishes fact sheets, reports on key issues, and the IMF annual report.

National Employment Law Project (NELP)

75 Maiden Lane, Suite 601, New York, NY   10038
(212) 285-3025 • fax: (212) 285-3044
e-mail: nelp@nelp.org
website: www.nelp.org

The National Employment Law Project (NELP) works to promote policies and programs that create good jobs, strengthen upward mobility, enforce worker rights, and help unemployed workers regain their economic footing through improved benefits and services. NELP develops and tests new policies at the state and local level, and then scales them up to spur change at the national level. Among the publications available at its website is "Scarring Effects: Demographics of the Long-Term Unemployed and the Danger of Ignoring the Jobs Deficit."

Organisation for Economic Co-operation and Development (OECD)

2, rue André Pascal, Paris Cedex 16   75775
   France
(33) 45 24 82 00 • fax: (33) 45 24 85 00
website: www.oecd.org

The Organisation for Economic Co-operation and Development (OECD) works to improve the economic and social well-being of people around the world. The OECD is a membership organization of thirty-four advanced and emerging countries around the world that work to foster prosperity worldwide. The OECD publishes economic surveys and health policy studies about individual nations and studies comparing countries, including numerous entries within its Society at a Glance series.

Peter G. Peterson Institute for International Economics

1750 Massachusetts Avenue NW, Washington, DC   20036
(202) 328-9000 • fax: (202) 659-3225
e-mail: comments@petersoninstitute.org
website: www.iie.com

The Peter G. Peterson Institute for International Economics is a private, nonprofit, nonpartisan research institution devoted to the study of international economic policy. The institute seeks to provide timely and objective analysis of, and concrete solutions to, a wide range of international economic problems. The institute publishes numerous policy briefs available at its website, including "How Europe Can Muddle Through Its Crisis."

Society for International Development (SID)

Via Panisperna 207, Rome   00184
   Italy
(39) 64872172 • fax: (39) 64872170
website: www.sidint.net

The Society for International Development (SID) is a global network of individuals and institutions concerned with development that is participative, pluralistic, and sustainable. SID aims to facilitate dialogue and help build consensus between various stakeholders and interest groups through its programs and initiatives. SID publishes several reports, including "The Middle Path: Towards Sustainability and Global Well-Being."

World Bank

1818 H Street NW, Washington, DC   20433
(202) 473-1000 • fax: (202) 477-6391
website: www.worldbank.org

The World Bank is made up of two unique development institutions owned by 187 member countries: the International Bank for Reconstruction and Development (IBRD) and the International Development Association (IDA). The World Bank provides low-interest loans, interest-free credits, and grants to developing countries for a wide array of purposes. The World Bank publishes the annual World Development Report and World Development Indicators.

World Economic Forum

91-93 route de la Capite, Cologny/Geneva   CH-1223
   Switzerland
(41) 22 869 1212 • fax: (41) 22 786 2744
e-mail: contact@weforum.org
website: www.weforum.org

The World Economic Forum is an independent international organization committed to improving the state of the world by engaging leaders in partnerships to shape global, regional, and industry agendas. The World Economic Forum has no political or national interests and holds annual meetings and other meetings among world leaders. The World Economic Forum publishes annual reports, global risk reports, and events reports, including "The Global Economic Burden of Non-Communicable Diseases."

Bibliography of Books

Lewis F. Abbot — *Theories of the Labour Market and Employment: A Review of the Social Science Literature.* Manchester, England: Industrial Systems Research, 1980.

Samir Amine, ed. — *Labor Markets: Dynamics, Trends and Economic Impact.* Hauppauge, NY: Nova Science Publishers, 2011.

Joyce Appleby — *The Relentless Revolution: A History of Capitalism.* New York: W.W. Norton, 2010.

Bruce Bartlett — *The New American Economy: The Failure of Reaganomics and a New Way Forward.* New York: Palgrave Macmillan, 2009.

Günseli Berik, Yana van der Meulen Rodgers, and Ann Zammit, eds. — *Social Justice and Gender Equality: Rethinking Development Strategies and Macroeconomic Policies.* New York: Routledge, 2009.

Ian Bremmer — *The End of the Free Market: Who Wins the War Between States and Corporations?* New York: Portfolio, 2010.

Jim Clifton — *The Coming Jobs War: What Every Leader Must Know About the Future of Job Creation.* New York: Gallup Press, 2011.

Carl Davidson and Steven J. Matusz	*International Trade with Equilibrium Unemployment.* Princeton, NJ: Princeton University Press, 2010.
Vox Day	*The Return of the Great Depression.* Los Angeles, CA: WND Books, 2009.
Melvyn Dubofsky and Foster Rhea Dulles	*Labor in America: A History.* Wheeling, IL: Harlan Davidson, 2010.
Gary S. Fields	*Working Hard, Working Poor: A Global Journey.* New York: Oxford University Press, 2012.
Jordi Galí	*Unemployment Fluctuations and Stabilization Policies: A New Keynesian Perspective.* Cambridge, MA: MIT Press, 2011.
Julius G. Getman	*Restoring the Power of Unions: It Takes a Movement.* New Haven, CT: Yale University Press, 2010.
Steven Hill	*Europe's Promise: Why the European Way Is the Best Hope in an Insecure Age.* Berkeley: University of California Press, 2010.
Thomas F. Huertas	*Crisis: Cause, Containment and Cure.* New York: Palgrave Macmillan, 2011.
David Hulme	*Global Poverty: How Global Governance Is Failing the Poor.* New York: Routledge, 2010.

Dean Karlan and Jacob Appel — *More than Good Intentions: How a New Economics Is Helping to Solve Global Poverty*. New York: Dutton, 2011.

Paul Krugman — *The Return of Depression Economics and the Crisis of 2008*. New York: W.W. Norton, 2009.

Richard Layard and Stephen J. Nickell — *Combatting Unemployment*. Eds. Werner Eichhorst and Klaus F. Zimmermann. New York: Oxford University Press, 2011.

Luis F. Felipe López-Calva and Nora Lustig, eds. — *Declining Inequality in Latin America: A Decade of Progress?* Washington, DC: Brookings Institution Press, 2010.

Michael J. Murray and Mathew Forstater — *The Job Guarantee: Toward True Full Employment*. New York: Palgrave Macmillan, 2013.

Richard A. Posner — *A Failure of Capitalism: The Crisis of '08 and the Descent into Depression*. Cambridge, MA: Harvard University Press, 2009.

Jack Rasmus — *Epic Recession: Prelude to Global Depression*. New York: Pluto Press, 2010.

Jay W. Richards — *Money, Greed, and God: Why Capitalism Is the Solution and Not the Problem*. New York: HarperOne, 2009.

Thomas E. Woods Jr.   *Meltdown: A Free-Market Look at Why the Stock Market Collapsed, the Economy Tanked, and Government Bailouts Will Make Things Worse.* Washington, DC: Regnery Publishing, 2009.

Michael D. Yates   *Why Unions Matter.* New York: Monthly Review Press, 2009.

Index

Geographic headings and page numbers in **boldface** refer to viewpoints about that country or region.

CPSIA information can be obtained
at www.ICGtesting.com
Printed in the USA
FFOW01n2137100414
4822FF